Endoı

Over the eight years of relationship with Sal, I have found him to be a man of vision and integrity. His passion for relationship with God and to find and define his destiny has been heartwarming and refreshing to me. This book comes out of the passion I have watched God refine in him. Over these years of refinement of integrity and character, he has grown in clarity and understanding of God's call on his life. This book is the product of many things: God working in Sal's life, his teachable spirit, and what He has learned from personal experience and through other mature and godly men. I highly recommend both the man and the book to those who desire to find and know God's destiny for their lives.
— **Dr. Wm. J. Hurst**
President, The Institute for Strategic Christian Leadership

God has an amazing plan for your life! In his book, Sal lays out this inescapable truth. His transparency and honesty about his own journey to the destiny God has for him is an inspiration to us all. I've known Sal for several years and have watched his journey to walk in God's call on his life; I have seen his passionate heart for God and his willingness to humble himself in obedience, allowing God to mature him so he could sustain the destiny God has set before him. This book exudes hope on every page—your destiny is waiting!
— **Rev. Linda Forster, M.A.**
Director, Healing the Heart Ministries, Life Center Ministries International

When I first met Sal Cerra, I immediately noticed that he was a gentle and compassionate man. He paid attention to those around him and was genuinely concerned with what others had to say to him. As I got to know him through working as an author coach on his first book, I soon realized that this wasn't just an ordinary man; but instead, a true man of God, one who is anointed to serve the body of Christ in power and wisdom. On several occasions I found myself both intrigued and extremely impressed with some of the topics that Sal and I discussed. Sal knows the Bible well and he is in love with Jesus. Sal is both kind-

loving and authentic. I fully recommend him; he is one of the truest forms of people who love the Lord without having a hidden agenda.
— **Andy Sanders**
International Writer, www.andysanders-writer.com

DESTINY
Dreams

DISCOVERING THE DIVINE BLUEPRINT FOR YOUR LIFE

SAL CERRA

I dedicate this book to Dr. Ann Trozzolillo, a mighty woman of God who has learned to walk in a love affair with Jesus. I've had the privilege of knowing Ann for many years throughout her ministry. Through the years, I have witnessed her obedience and faithfulness to the assignment God has placed on her heart. Ann has a passion for seeing people set free. Her fire for God has facilitated a revival in the hearts of many. Ann is a living testament of walking into the fullness and seeing her God-ordained destiny come into completeness.

I thank the Lord for bringing this wonderful, amazing woman into my life. She has been an incredible influence over my life, and I am honored to call her "Mom." Thank you, Ann, for all that you have sown into the kingdom of God. The seeds you have planted and nourished will be seen in an abundant harvest. I can only imagine what God has promised for you in heaven someday. Your reward will be unimaginable!

Love,

Your boy, Sal

CONTENTS

FOREWORD

Although the word *destiny* is not found in the Bible, the word *predestination* is recorded in several passages of scripture. *Predestination* means that God has a purpose that is determined long before it is brought to pass. It implies that God is infinitely capable of planning and then bringing about what He has planned. (See Isaiah 14:24–27; 41:7; 46:9–10; Jeremiah 29:11–14; and Ephesians 1:4–5).

Several years ago, I had the opportunity to meet Sal Cerra when he met and married the daughter of a very close friend of mine. Over these past few years, I've had the privilege of working with Sal and his wife on their spiritual journey. In this book, Sal shares his experiences and encounters that helped awaken him to the reality of destiny. His story shows us that all of our experiences—the good, bad, and ugly or hurtful—are used by God, assuring us that everything is redeemable (working all things together for our good).

Destiny Dreams inspires us to see that the people, places, and things, as well as the *order* of our life, aligns with the Master's plan. When we go off the "designated route," our divine "recalculate button" is hit to reset us. We do not have to go searching for our destiny; we see that if we simply fulfill our routine responsibilities and attach the acknowledgment of the "God-factor," we are able to intersect the natural to the supernatural to awaken to destiny (see the story in 1 Samuel 9:3–5 and 9:20).

Some will have an encounter. Others will just go about daily responsibilities—but both will ultimately see destiny fulfilled. The apostle Paul says it best in Philippians 3:13: "Brethren, I do not count myself to have apprehended but one thing, I do forget those things which are behind and reaching forward to those things which are ahead."

Destiny Dreams will enlighten and inform the reader that there is a customized life that God has ordained, and He will equip you to accomplish it to bring Him the greatest glory and achieve the maximum expansion of His kingdom. In this book, Sal gives us a checklist to enable us to practice the presence of God. These practical applications help us to secure a life of fulfillment.

Destiny Dreams invites us to learn to grow and walk with God so that we know our identity and increase in our intimacy with Him. We not only want to know about Him, but to *know* Him, His ways, and His heart.

— Aaron Evans
The Emerging Daniel Company

Intimacy with the Father is the
most rewarding treasure.

~ Sal Cerra

PREFACE

T he Father's love is undeniably one of the most precious gifts of all. His love for you comes in the purest form that anyone could ever give or receive. The love that the Father gives is something that everyone wants to experience; He desires you! He wants to spend quality time with you. His love, from the heart of God, is a gift that you can have and experience for the rest of your life. Yes, His love truly is a gift—and that means it isn't earned and you don't have to work to receive it. It has been there all along.

God's love doesn't elevate or increase for you when you are good. The same goes for when you're bad; His love doesn't diminish toward you because you are a bad person. No, His love is completely perfect in every way. That means that it will always remain constant for you.

You Can't Earn God's Love

The Father's love isn't based on merit. It's not something that you can or can't do for someone. In our human experience, it is normal to have to do something so another person will either accept us or not be upset with us, but that is not how love works with God. Once we cross over into the mentality of "I've got to earn this Father's love," it turns into earned love, which is no longer pure. He loves you and me, regardless! He's not ninety-nine percent for you and one percent upset—He's one-hundred percent fully sold out and committed to you. He was for you in the past, He is for you now, and He will always be. Is this how you see the Father's love for you?

13

There is a quality to God's love that causes it to never diminish. How does it work? Think about the worst thing imaginable that you have ever done in your life. Now realize that during the time when you were doing that awful thing, God's love was still right there for you. His love for you never wavered—and it still remains constant. It will never weaken toward you under any circumstance.

Society teaches us that we have to earn the Father's love, it's the way the world works. We have to work to earn pay; we work to progress in life. If we're not careful, we carry over this same mentality and apply it to our relationship with God and end up working hard to try to develop a relationship with God. I'm not talking about commitment and dedication. There's nothing wrong with commitment. Being dedicated to anything in life will demand hard work. Great relationships require great commitment, time, and effort. *But we can't approach our relationship with God like this.*

In God's perfect will and love there isn't error, shame, dishonor, or disregard for who you are as a person.

When it comes to determination and accomplishing our goals in life, I believe in hard work because I've seen the benefit of it through working with my father in the construction business. Hard work produces a lot of good things. I support being committed to the body of Christ and I understand that it will require effort and work. Someone has to turn the lights on and take out the trash when we meet to worship the Lord. Again, I'm not against commitment, discipline, and determination. I'm for hard work in everything that I do because it's the right thing to have in your life. I've seen the impact of lazy people and the outcome of their life. Sadly, I've seen what they could have become, but probably won't because they weren't dedicated to their cause in life. If you want to accomplish anything in life you must be dedicated.

Hard work, however, won't cause the Father to love you any more than He already does. God's love doesn't require work, because He loves you more than life itself. You are the only thing, being, or substance that has ever been made in His image—you were designed in the Father's image! You're made in the perfect will of the Father. Yes, you are made in the Father's love. In God's perfect will and love there isn't error, shame, dishonor, or disregard for who you are as a person. No other creature can ever say that about the love of the Father toward them. That is how deep God's love runs for you. You are His treasured possession.

Receiving the Gift

When something is given to you as a gift, you don't have to earn it—ever! It's freely given and freely received. When the gifts are given out at Christmas time, there isn't a contingency to receive those gifts, or at least there shouldn't be. Have you ever had someone hold out a gift to you at Christmas and then state a task you had to accomplish in order to get to open it? Sounds crazy, right? Someone who loves and cares for you gave you that gift, and it was just that—a gift. In the same way, you didn't look at the tag and read something like this: "This is only your gift as long as I approve of you. The moment I no longer approve of you, I will take this gift back." That would be absurd!

Sadly, that is how the world operates and it is how society teaches us to live. Even worse, that is sometimes how the church operates. It's easy to assume that because someone is active in the church that their relationship with God is going really well. But that isn't how it works. Service for the Lord doesn't equal intimacy with Jesus. There are many well-meaning people with good hearts who have "bitten" that lie; they took that apple and choked on it. We have seen it happen: Someone starts a passionate walk with the Lord, and before long they exchange their once-pure relationship with God for doing acts of service in the church. They lost their first love. This can happen to anyone. Perhaps this has happened to you or someone you love. It is really common nowadays because there is so much stress on being productive, which can be interpreted to mean that we can find acceptance through working

15

hard and being a good contributor to society. The world tells us that if we do these things, then we are accepted, and if we're important, then we are loved. That is a completely false way of thinking.

The gifts that you received over the years from people who love you were given out of the deep love that the giver had for you. We've all experienced getting a gift from someone who didn't expect anything in return; their affection and joy was evident when you opened it and saw that wonderful gift that they put so much thought into. They gave that gift to you because they love and care for you. In the same way, we have all given gifts to others out of the goodness of our heart, not to get something back. Now multiply that a zillion times over, and then keep adding even more zeroes to the end—that is a picture of the Father's love for you! That is how much He wants to be with you. God's love for you is free; consequently, His passion for you is overflowing and never ends. He earnestly wants you!

Sometimes we work so hard trying to please the Father that we forget that He is already well pleased with us.

The Father's adoration toward you is effortless on your part. His love is unconditionally yours—always. People may try to say otherwise. The church may even attempt to teach us that we have to earn the Father's love by working and serving hard within the church walls. You know, like filling our schedules up with a "do this" or "do that" list in order to get closer to the Lord. What I think happens in the church is that sometimes we work so hard trying to please the Father that we forget that He is already well pleased with us. He is pleased with you already! He is happy to be with you and to come near you. God, the Creator of the universe, wants you more than anything else that He created. You have become "pre-earned" with God. That's right! You can't earn His love for you. It's impossible to earn something that is unattainable through works. Working harder or working less won't cause God to love you more or less. It's been earned, freely given to you. How does it work? It's like an unlimited line of credit, but better; you are pre-approved for God's love. His love for you was pre-determined, preexisting, and, in reality, you didn't have to earn it at all. It's there, never changing.

So how can we change our way of thinking when it comes to God's love for us? When we start to talk like this, we eventually start thinking like this, and the end result is that we start to believe it—we actually start to comprehend that God has an unyielding love for us. He has an unwavering love for you and me that will never fade. That is His deepest passion—to love you!

Have you ever felt like someone was against you? You could tell that they didn't like you for whatever reason. Maybe they chose to cut you off for something that they heard about you; and whether it was true or not, they chose to believe it and prematurely judged you. Unfortunately, this has happened to all of us at one time or another and it can be very painful. Betrayal hurts!

Now flip this concept over to the other side for a moment. Has someone ever really been on your side for no apparent reason? Maybe you needed help and this person stepped up to help you. They didn't have to be your advocate; they had no strings attached to your situation, but they chose to stop what they were doing and become the solution to your problem. Their world was just fine while yours was falling apart, and they came to your rescue like a knight in shining armor or someone with great influence. They stopped everything they were doing to fight for you. At the end of the battle, they didn't ask for anything at all. They don't want your money, a thank-you card, or anything. Nope! They did it because they were moved by compassion for you and your circumstance. That is how God is toward you. Regardless of who you are or what you have done, this is that love! It is the Father's love—an all-original, undying, unquenchable fire burning for you.

There is a deep well of love longing to be near you. He wants to be close to you much more than you can ever realize. He wants to be close to us more than we want to be close to Him. His love will penetrate the

17

darkest of evil and the loneliest of nights. He can remove your worst memories. What makes us whole and functional is having the Father's love as the center of our life. The "wholeness" of His love for you is found in the fact that the very essence of God is complete love and passion. You see, Jesus is a God of grace, mercy, judgment, justice, forgiveness, commitment, stability, honor, integrity—the list goes on and on and on. Mixed through all of that is His love, which is the purest form of love ever! That is what creates the wholeness of who you are. He loves you more than anyone could ever attempt to write or explain to you.

The Father's love for you; that is what I'm talking about. I'm writing this book to express to you that His love is deeper, wider, and more pleasurable than anything you could ever imagine. He loves YOU! You might be asking, "I thought this book was about destiny. Why are you talking so much about God's love?" With love comes destiny. We can only understand our destiny when we fully understand the Father's love for us. You will never walk in the fullness of your destiny until you grasp the fullness of Christ and His love, living in you and working through you. His adoration toward you is endless; His passion for you is infinite. What He wants to do for you and through you are far greater than you can imagine.

Hidden Treasures

God's love and desire for you is what creates your destiny. Just like His love was already there for you, His destiny is also already right there, waiting for you. The destiny for your life—the divine blueprint—was already established, created, breathed into your DNA. For no one else but you! Nobody can ever fulfill the plan you have been given through the love of the Father.

When you were created, God made such a unique blueprint for your life that nobody else can use that exact one but you. And in case you haven't noticed or connected the pieces yet, this is a two-part deal with the Father. It's all His doing for you. You get His unconditional love—plus you get to walk in His perfect destiny for you. Both are right there, ready to be embraced. And there is so much more that the Father has waiting for you with His open arms. It's like jumping into the deepest river or well, and once you reach the bottom you discover that there are still miles and miles left to experience. The wells of God are limitless and they are right before you.

The depth of God's love is unsearchable, yet He allows us to search it out because He wants us to discover glorious treasures from the throne of grace. He is that good of a Father. Along the path of life, He willingly places hidden treasures throughout the trail. He doesn't hide the treasures so that you hopefully miss them or can't find them at all. NO! He hides things from us so we can seek them out. He wants us to discover them, which will cause us to treasure them much more than we would have if He just handed them to us. He wants you to find every gift and treasure that He has hidden for you so you can walk in them and experience His fullness as much as possible. God wants to play hide and seek with you to have fun with you.

> Again, the kingdom of heaven is like treasure hidden in a field, which a man found and hid; and for joy over it he goes and sells all that he has and buys that field (Matthew 13:44).

Back in this time period, keeping something valuable was hard to do. They didn't have banks, and there were plenty of thieves hanging around just waiting for an opportunity to steal that treasure away. If you put this in their perspective back then, it sheds a whole new light on this scripture. Today we can quickly build fences, train watchdogs, add cameras, and install alarms. By a quick click of a few buttons, the police are called. This wasn't the case in ancient Jewish culture. If you were a peasant or someone other than a king, you probably didn't have guards near you, and you definitely didn't have electric security alarms like we do now. So keeping something hidden was hard. The person who had something of value would often go out late at night while nobody was watching, and they would hide the treasure in a place where only they would know about. This was often done in a local field, usually in their own field or in a field that they labored in for their master. They did this

19

to protect the valuable treasure from thieves, but they also hid some of their most valuable possessions to protect their assets during war.

During a time of war, two things could happen:

Their own government could demand certain pay or "war relief funds" to go toward the government to fund the battle. If the government knew there was an enemy threat nearby and they felt that your property would be the next best outpost, they had the right to seize your property. With your treasure hidden, they couldn't just seize it along with the property.

The other thing that could happen if a war broke out in your region was the potential for enemy countries to take over your land. With the treasures hidden underground, they wouldn't know where your most valuable treasures were.

When you see all of this in the context for the time in which it was written, can you see how common it would be to hide valuables in a field? So the emphasis in this scripture isn't on the person who found the treasure; it's on the fact that the treasure was found. God loves you so much that He is willing to hide treasures from heaven within fields. He knows that one day you will dig into it to find it. We may call them "miracles," but God calls them "treasures" from His heart to you. They are gifts sent from above.

I would like to point something else out here. The person who found the valuable treasure didn't even own the field. Did you catch that? We don't know why he was digging; some suggest that he was a laborer, one out working in his master's fields somewhere. This isn't certain. But one thing is sure—the man who found the treasure knew Jewish law and was also a "smart cookie." Back in this time, if you bought a field, you also purchased everything that remained in the field, both on top of it and beneath the ground as well. So why did he cover the treasure back up? He did this to stop others from finding it, to keep bandits away, and to keep the current owner from discovering this information. He quickly went and bought the field, thus purchasing the treasure hidden in the field that, most likely, was worth more than the whole field itself.

So what's the point?

God doesn't hide things to keep them *from you*; He hides them *for you to discover*. Once you discover the treasures, He then wants to bless you lavishly. This laborer in the Bible probably had a complete life-style change once he purchased the field and dug up the hidden treasure. God chose to bless the laborer by helping him walk into his destiny. The future of your destiny is always much greater than you can ever imagine because your destiny has the mark of the Father's love all over it.

That is what this book is about: Destiny dreaming for you. Your destiny is found through the amazing love of the Father's heart toward you. His embrace is always warm, His smile at you is always welcoming, and His desire for you is always burning with a deep love that will never be quenched. That is the promise of the love of the Father and how He desires to give you a most precious gift—His destiny for you.

> # God doesn't hide things to keep them *from you*; He hides them *for you to discover.*

He wants you to succeed in life. He wants you to accomplish all that He has ever asked you to set out and do. This isn't about just checking off a list or doing something very well. If God could choose, the greatest thing you could ever accomplish is to be conformed into the image of His Son, Jesus Christ. And the only way to be conformed into the image of His Son is to spend time in His presence and get to know His ways. More than anything on earth, He wants to be with you. He loves you much more than anyone else can ever dream or imagine. His presence is "empty" without your presence near. That's right! He wants you! God wants to be near you all the time. It's like a passionate love affair with Jesus. You leave what the world says it can offer you and then He invites you to His throne to be in His presence. He embraces you with real, genuine compassion. He cuddles you with His warm heart—the love of the Father. And when He touches your heart, you will *never* forget it! He loves and cares for you that much.

His love and destiny come with His presence. He longs for you to be in His presence. He desires to be near you. More than anything else, what the Father wants is to see His perfect will for your life be completed. This is something that is already secured for you. He wants to say, "Well done, good and faithful servant." He also says, "I love you! I deeply love you more than anything else."

This is destiny dreaming for you. This is destiny crying out louder than any sound ever created before. This is God calling you to a higher ground, a higher romance with Him. God, the King of Romance, is here to awaken your soul.

What you're about to read is a divine romance between you and an awesome God! You'll understand how to have an authentic love affair with Jesus. He wants to zealously experience you, and better yet, He wants you to experience Him. This is destiny dreaming for you!

INTRODUCTION

T he Lord is so good to His people. He never wants trouble or conflict to take the place of peace and blessing in the lives of people. God always desires to heal the broken-hearted and see them restored. This is what He has been doing for me.

There was a season in my life when things weren't going too well. I was arguing with someone I once loved, and getting nowhere fast in resolving the issues that we were facing. My household was a mess, and I was doing the best I could to turn all of it around—and nothing was working. It seemed as though everything in my life—everything dear to me—was coming to a close; a dead end without my permission. I knew God was there somewhere, but during this time it was like He was silent or asleep concerning my problems. I would hear about others being blessed or I would read about how God came through for someone in some bizarre way to bring breakthrough in some amazing, supernatural way. For whatever reason, nothing was moving right in my life. And to make matters worse, people around me could clearly see it. Some people could tell that something serious was about to happen and that the outcome would probably not favor my decisions or wishes at all. I felt like my life was in a tunnel where each day dragged on into the next and so on. That went on for a year. Each week was a big ball of mess that morphed into one huge blurred state of chaos. If my life was a ship, then it would have been sinking fast. Or if that particular year was an airplane, I would have been spinning completely out of control over the ocean.

Have you ever been in a situation that felt like the more you prayed about something, the worse it got? That was my life several years ago. I was desperate for God to move. I was begging and crying out to God for a breakthrough. Sometimes desperation will cause you to do practically anything to get through the mess you're in. I was moving in that direction; I wanted to see God do what He does best—perform a miracle when I needed it most.

What Is Desperation?

What does it mean to be desperate? The dictionary calls *Desperation* this: "A state of despair, or utter hopelessness; reckless fury."[1]

You can probably think of at least a few moments in your life where you felt just like I did at that hopeless point in my life. I can undoubtedly see the connection between desperation and making rash decisions or extreme behavior. Life-threatening situations require extreme decisions, and if we are honest with ourselves, we will admit that we don't always handle bad situations the right way.

Whether the definition above is correct or not, I see a different point of view with the word *desperation*. As a Christian, I like to look at it through the eyes of a person covered by the blood of Jesus. This helps me understand that I've been in His hand the entire time. God makes no mistakes in our lives! It's interesting that when we experience something firsthand and then look back on it, we can define it in our own words. This is because we have lived it, walked through it, and watched God get us out of it. With this in mind, here might be a clearer definition of the word *desperation*:

> *Desperation*: When everything has fallen apart and nothing or no one will help you.

It's at this moment when you fall to your knees and cry out to a Holy God who is above all creation on earth. At this exact moment, you will

---

1. *Webster's Collegiate Dictionary*, s.v., "desperation," (G. & C Merriam Co.: Springfield, 1913). Public Domain.

discover that Jesus was listening, waiting, and revealing His plan all along. God's arms are wide open and His thoughts are always directed toward you. This is how destiny is discovered.

For me, my tragedy was turned into the Lord's triumph! And it was when I desperately needed God to work on my behalf. At the time, I was screaming to God, yet all I heard back from Him was silence. Looking back, now I know that He wasn't silent at all—He was setting up divine intervention through the chaos of my desperation. That is what produced the activation of destiny over my life.

The seeds of destiny are already within you...you just haven't discovered them yet.

Whether you see them or not, the seeds of destiny are already within you. That's right, they are right there waiting for you; you just haven't discovered them yet. While all of the mess in my life was happening and nothing appeared to be working, I was only seeing the situation through my eyes—my lens. But God was watching from above, waiting for His perfect timing to unfold. That is the Father's will for you. He wants to unfold His best timing and blessings right before your eyes. If you don't hear or see Him right now, don't lose hope; He will respond in a way that will be mind-blowing!

While I was going through this time in my life, I had been having a lot of dreams. Some dreams seemed to speak right into the realm of where I was and what I was walking through at that moment. Other dreams I just couldn't seem to understand or make out. But God was speaking through both types of dreams in ways and levels that would change the course of my life and relationship with Him forever. Things were rapidly falling apart in my life. A relationship that I was in was not doing well, and I didn't know what else to do. Sometimes in life, two people are really trying to make things work, but they are still heading in the opposite directions. That was the case for me.

At that moment, while I thought my life was going through endless barrages of disaster, God saw it as a divine opportunity to intervene. At my wits' end, I ended up in a hotel at six o'clock in the morning, crying on the floor of my room. Suddenly the atmosphere shifted, but I couldn't tell exactly what was happening. I grabbed my Bible and began to read this passage:

> Therefore I also, after I heard of your faith in the Lord Jesus and your love for all the saints, do not cease to give thanks for you, making mention of you in my prayers: that the God of our Lord Jesus Christ, the Father of glory, may give to you the spirit of wisdom and revelation in the knowledge of Him, the eyes of your understanding being enlightened; that you may know what is the hope of His calling, what are the riches of the glory of His inheritance in the saints, and what *is* the exceeding greatness of His power toward us who believe, according to the working of His mighty power which He worked in Christ when He raised Him from the dead and seated *Him* at His right hand in the heavenly *places,* far above all principality and power and might and dominion, and every name that is named, not only in this age but also in that which is to come. And He put all *things* under His feet, and gave Him *to be* head over all *things* to the church, which is His body, the fullness of Him who fills all in all. (Ephesians 1:15–23)

Instantly, something started happening to me—my body was still there in that hotel room, but I wasn't there. I was having a real out-of-body experience. I found myself in the presence of the King of Glory. It was completely supernatural and like a sci-fi movie, but better—this was God's divine destiny exploding in my life! This was something I will never forget the rest of my life.

I was literally soaring! I had an all-access, supernatural flight scheduled just for me by the King of kings. Don't you love it when God decides to break "code" with man-made regulations and structure?

That's what He did for me that day. I was literally soaring by the Spirit. He had taken total control, and there I was, having one-on-one time with Jesus up in the sky. That moment was far better than any drug or chemical that you can ever abuse. I know; I've been on drugs before. Drugs diminish; precious times with Jesus never fade.

Then it got even better!

> # Instantly, something started happening to me—my body was still there in that hotel room, but I wasn't there. I was having a real out-of-body experience.

What's happening now? I thought. While I was soaring in the skies above, I noticed a rather distinct shift in the atmosphere. I soon realized that I wasn't just up in the skies—the clouds, if you will—I was starting to ascend straight up. It was like I was going up toward heaven, like a rocket gliding through the atmosphere or space. That's pretty awesome! It takes nearly 18,000 miles per hour for a rocket to accelerate fast enough to achieve orbit. I didn't have a speedometer on me that day (and not that it matters), but when we are "caught up in the Spirit," just how fast are we going? I'm not exactly sure, but I was moving rather quickly! This split-second divine moment in time was completely breathtaking for me to experience.

While I was ascending, the only way I can describe it is that it was like I was going up and in and out of a rock and stone maze. It was something I've never seen before, and I'm not exactly sure what it was. Whatever it was, God ordained it to take place. Before long, I was moving out of the stone maze and right back into the sky where I could see Jesus. There He was in all of His glory! How beautiful was that moment. One moment I was crying on the floor of a hotel room in utter desperation, and now I was moving through the skies, rapidly approaching Jesus. As I got closer to Jesus, I could see a throne behind Him. When He moved,

His throne moved with Him. Eternal glory encircled Him; nothing was near Him without permission. Then I noticed that around the throne was a mass of different creatures all around it. Both "holy" and "glorious" are two words that come to mind when I think back on that encounter.

When you are in a divinely-appointed visitation like that, you're not thinking of your problems or how they will unfold, good or bad. You are thinking about Him, the Master and Savior of the world, Jesus Christ! I soon discovered that time, space, and distances aren't the same in the presence of God. Why is this? Time and distance have a much different meaning in the presence of Jesus because we are in an eternal time clock. It could have felt like five minutes, but in God's time table, five minutes can actually be five hours. Imagine what it will be like in heaven—in eternity—with perfected bodies without sin, sickness, and death. It gets me excited just thinking about it. I can't wait!

> Now I saw a new heaven and a new earth, for the first
> heaven and the first earth had passed away. Also there
> was no more sea. (Revelation 21:1)

When we are in the heavenlies, things will change, and what God chooses to do when we are near Him is far beyond what someone can write in the pages of a single book. Life-changing encounters will alter your life for the remainder of your time on earth, and it often opens up more divine encounters once you are back on earth. When I was up in the heavenlies with Jesus, I could see Him on a holy throne that was suspended in midair, like I was. I couldn't see other people; everything in me was focused on Jesus. While my situation had not yet changed, my perspective changed—and that made all the difference! God ambushed my desperation; I no longer feared my future. The perfect love of Christ cast out all of my fears and worries. I was in the sky, but life's turmoil and the toll that it had taken on my mind and body were both completely gone. It was right then and there when destiny kissed my desperation goodbye. I immediately knew what God was asking me to do with my life.

That is how God works; that is how much He loves us. He is willing to call us out and up in order to rearrange our lives down on earth. That is what He did for me, and it's what He is eager to do for you if needed. Once I came back down from heaven, I started having more out-of-body experiences, and more visions and dreams would soon follow. That encounter with Jesus opened up a divine funnel filled with His Spirit into my being. These encounters have continued from that day forward.

What is all of this? It's destiny manifesting, taking control of what was once out of control. When God speaks words of destiny into your life, the lesser becomes the greater as the incomplete areas of our lives are made completely whole. Destiny will take a beggar and turn them into a king. Destiny is always working for you—never working against you.

> # Destiny is a course correction or course shift in life. It is when God steps in and changes our direction.

Destiny Will Remove Laziness from You

> The hand of the diligent will rule, but the lazy *man* will be put to forced labor. (Proverbs 12:24)

Destiny is a course correction or course shift in life. It is when God steps in and changes our direction. Right then and there we have to act on it, prepare, move out, and trust the Lord. When God gives us a mandate, call, and purpose for life, He is asking us to accomplish it. For some people, that might mean that you have to walk out this journey alone for a while. I think one of the most dangerous things to do in life is throw your responsibility off on someone else. I'm not referring to hiring someone else to do a job for you because you don't have the proper skills to finish something or because they can do a better job in a more timely manner.

My father and I dealt with this all the time when we were building houses to sell. Sometimes it was better to hire a different contractor for the concrete work and another one for the framing job, and then our team would come in after those professionals were finished to add the remaining parts and finishing touches. Other times, our work crew would handle the entire house building project from the ground up. Each house was built differently and had different situations and scenarios we had to work through. Two houses that look exactly alike on the outside could be treated very differently because they were two distinct and completely separate homes.

> # Your calling might be similar to someone else's, but it is still different than any other calling out there because only you can fulfill the parts of your destiny the way God created you to accomplish it.

Your calling might be similar to someone else's, but it is still different than any other calling out there because only you can fulfill the parts of your destiny the way God created you to accomplish it. Others might be able to get their destiny accomplished better, quicker, and with more accuracy, but nobody can fill the exact shoes that you are called to walk in. That is what your destiny is all about. As Christians, we can't just toss our destiny off to the side and expect others to do all of the work for us; we can't fulfill God's calling without having to sacrifice anything. Just picture Noah in the Bible for a moment.

> Thus Noah did; according to all that God commanded him, so he did. (Genesis 6:22)

What does this mean?

For starters, Noah had to build an ark (boat) which took him roughly 120 years or so. Imagine dedicating a large portion of your life to building just one thing, but doing it for the Lord and getting it done properly the first time. There wasn't a "Plan B" in this equation for Noah. If the first boat didn't work, Noah couldn't return it to the store. And if Noah decided that he didn't want to do the work and asked his neighbor to build the boat for him while he went off and did something different with his life, it wouldn't have worked out so well for Noah. When the rains came, Noah would have ended up as a "floater" along with the rest of mankind.

Secondly, Noah had to build a boat to float on rain waters that never existed prior to this. The Bible tells us that the floods burst forth from the grounds and the floodgates from heaven came forth (Gen. 7:11). That means that up until this moment on earth, it had never rained before; thus, the gravity density was much lower, making it possible for people to live much longer. So our man, Noah, was building an oversized raft to withstand floodwaters that nobody on earth had ever experienced before. Talk about blind faith! Noah did everything God had said to do, including herding every single species of animal, two-by-two, along with providing food and safety for every person and creature in the boat. He had to make sure that one of the lions didn't eat one of the sheep, and so on.

Noah did it! He did all that the Lord wanted him to accomplish and he did it by faith.

> By faith Noah, being divinely warned of things not yet seen, moved with godly fear, prepared an ark for the saving of his household, by which he condemned the world and became heir of the righteousness which is according to faith. (Hebrews 11:7)

Sometimes destiny isn't flashy—it's just hidden obedience. That is how destiny works, and that is how it will work in your life. As Christians, we must learn how to walk in the Spirit each day, putting Him first in all that we do. This is learning how to listen to the Father's love, trusting Him more than ever before, and embracing the gifts that He has for us. This is destiny dreaming for you!

CHAPTER 1: SEEKING GOD IN THE CHAOS

L et's fast forward. There she was—her life was completely upended. Mine was broken into too many damaged parts. Both of our worlds were encircled with some of the darkest and most challenging moments of our lives—and right in the middle of it all, God chose to break through. Breakthrough is when "destiny" steps in and allows you to leap forward. For me, it was when I saw her for the very first time. She walked through the door. She was a wreck. I had no idea who she was. It didn't matter—my life was in complete turmoil. For her, it was when I stepped into the prayer circle and said, "Jesus loves you." She looked up and our eyes connected for the first time. She told me later that something happened in that moment. Something in her soul stirred, but she was not ready—and neither was I. God was sovereignly connecting two different people with two very different, yet similarly challenging life stories. As I look back now, I realize that God was doing something supernatural from the very first time we ever met. It was almost a year until we saw each other again. I had no idea what God had been doing in her life since we'd first laid eyes on each other. This is her story, in her words:

> I had lost my husband to cancer after twenty-six years of marriage. I was heartbroken. I always believed that God would bring restoration to me and my children. I had to learn to lean into Him and let go of my fears.

To trust Him completely. As months went by, my life started to explode. Things started happening in my life that I had never experienced before. I started to become more "aware" of God's voice and His presence in my life. I started having dreams and visions about the man God was going to bring into my life. Through these revelations, God was showing me my future husband's pain and desperation. I started to intercede and pray for the situation God was revealing to me. I had no idea where this was going or who the man was in my dreams. I had to completely trust in God and what He was doing. As time went by, little by little, God started to reveal more and more of who the man might be. As God was speaking to me, His insight brought me back to that moment in time when my eyes connected to that person who once told me, "Jesus loves you." I went from complete despair to having a hope for my future. God was supernaturally preparing me for my destiny.

As God was moving and speaking in her life, He was also moving and speaking in mine. Our worlds collided once again. In the midst of it all, God was with us—ordaining every step, every decision. He was leading us down the road to destiny, our destiny as husband and wife.

Tragedy isn't the end of your life; it's the welcome mat for destiny to step forward.

Chaos Isn't God's Nature

What does chaos have to do with a person's destiny? I'm glad you asked that question because I believe the Bible gives us a really good answer. Merriam-Webster defines *chaos* as "the unorganized condition of mass or matter before the creation of distinct and orderly forms; any confused collection of things; disorder; confusion."[2]

2. *Webster's Collegiate Dictionary*, s.v., "chaos," (G. & C Merriam Co.: Springfield, 1913). Public Domain.

As you can see here, chaos isn't God's nature at all. He isn't unpredictable; rather, He is very predictable. Just look at how the Bible is written and laid out. If God was unpredictable, He wouldn't have written the Bible at all. He would have created everything and then destroyed it without any redemption or restoration plan. God doesn't have a "Plan B" because He doesn't make mistakes. He is that good, that consistent! I mean, come on, He spelled out exactly what He did, what He is going to do, and how it will all unfold throughout eternity. God is perfect love, and in that, all things were created, formed, and placed into proper order and timing. Nothing is with error once God gets ahold of it. Nothing—including your life—is ever put to waste in the hands of God. That is the love of the Father for you.

Tragedy isn't the end of your life; it's the welcome mat for destiny to step forward.

God is also never confused. He hasn't been confused even once in all of time. The Bible tells us that God isn't the author of confusion; Satan is.

For God is not the author of confusion but of peace, as in all the churches of the saints (1 Corinthians 14:33).

Think about this for a moment: If God isn't the creator of confusion and Satan is, then what does it mean when you or someone around you says that you/they are confused? It means that the person saying it isn't clearly hearing God's will for their life; they aren't totally walking in divine guidance from the Lord at that moment. They may be a Christian, but someone or something is persuading them in the *wrong* direction somehow. Satan uses this tactic when someone is starting to walk into their destiny. He will consistently throw something ahead of God's timing to throw you completely out of God's perfect will. Looking back in life and where I am now, I recognize that there were many times when God was getting ready to open a divine door for my life and something

35

else prematurely closed or opened that was out of God's timing. It almost caused me to nearly miss God's perfectly-timed door. Interestingly enough, God always came through in the end. That is destiny and that is how it works!

Rest assured that God has you right where He wants you. He is going to help you not only walk through your mess, but also to overcome it. He wants you to be able to share with others that you were in a serious situation in life and that He showed you how to deal with it—rendering your adversary helpless so the problems couldn't come back around a second or third time. He will show you how to break the curse and cycle forever! That is how destiny is formed. Destiny will help us overcome the assignments sent to destroy us. Destiny is formed when it looks like nothing good can come out of your situation. Destiny doesn't run *from* you but *toward* you.

> In the beginning God created the heavens and the earth. The earth was without form, and void; and darkness was on the face of the deep. And the Spirit of God was hovering over the face of the waters. (Genesis 1:1–2)

When we think of God creating something out of nothing, sometimes we assume that the "nothing" was darkness, like empty matter or some unknown substance filling space or time that was already in existence. However, that wasn't the case. God didn't create the universe out of something else, like a big atomic ball filled with blackest darkness. Instead, our magnificent God created something completely out of nothing. This means that He created everything from what is beyond darkness—complete nothingness! He worked past the state of total formlessness. Everything was void and nothing was there—not even air. How do we know this? Because darkness didn't exist before God; He has always existed, even before light and dark, air, molecules, substance, or matter was ever formed. As Creator, He formed it all—even you!

So what did God do next? After He looked over the surface of the deep (which is "nothing"), He took the formless matter and turned it into life for the first time ever. It's interesting to point out here that He didn't grab hold of darkness (nothing) and shake it into something with His strong hands. Instead, He *spoke* light right into the nothingness.

> Then God said, "Let there be light"; and there was light. And God saw the light, that it was good; and God divided the light from the darkness. God called the light Day, and the darkness He called Night. So the evening and the morning were the first day. (Genesis 1:3–5)

Now with this in mind, let's go back to "chaos" for a minute and connect it to our day-to-day lives. If you're old enough to know better, then you know that chaos doesn't ask for permission to strike, nor does it show up invited. Chaos will never get permission to be placed on your calendar. As bad as it may sound, chaos is the missing ingredient to a person's destiny. What we attempt to avoid as much as possible will eventually become the antidote to the sickness, or "sick of this mess" life that we are living in. As human beings, we often make every effort to avoid conflict or trouble—chaos, if you will. We don't want more problems attached to our life, and we certainly don't need anymore "to-do lists" added to our days. Yet our Father welcomes it because He already knows the outcome. What? Yes! *Our Father welcomes chaos.* He allows it because He knows that the trouble we walk through will eventually bring out the best in and through us. Our environment will hone the inside of our lives in such a way that the diamond tucked deep down inside of us will emerge and eventually be seen. This means that God has you right where He wants you.

If you're up in the North going through treacherous winters and can't stand them, believe me, God has you right where you're supposed to be right now. He might call you to another place sometime, but know that you are right where He wants you for this time in your life. Likewise, you may be in a warmer region, or different country; God also has His hand on your life right there in that hot location. When it comes to God and how He works all things out for His plan, your surroundings are just as much as a part of the divine destiny as what God is working on the inside of your life, including where you believe God is taking you one

37

day. If we aren't careful, we can get so caught up on "getting there" that we forget that God is also in the *now*. He wants us to enjoy the moment, the process, and the path that He has set in motion for our lives. There have been some times in my life where I would have rather had a flash forward into the next stage and season of my life, but God had me go all the way through the process from beginning to end—and that process was exactly what God used to change my life for the better on the inside. God is working on us on the *inside*. He is in the details—those things that matter most. He wants to use the outside environment, our surroundings, in order to work a divine well in our lives that holds the glory of God.

God isn't scared of your chaos; it's just the opposite. He is forging destiny out of it.

What I want you to understand through this book is that God isn't scared of your chaos; it's just the opposite. He is forging destiny out of it. Let me say it as simply as possible: God is in your Chaos! He doesn't cower in fear when He sees problems arise. He never turns down an opportunity to turn what was horrible into something that is amazing! God will not only outsmart your adversary; He will win every time. He is fighting for you, willing to love and cherish you much more than you realize. Destiny is a personal blessing from the Father to you.

Just look at my own life. Who would have ever thought that anything good could have come out of the chaos I created? But God never wastes an opportunity. He uses both the bad and the good to bring about His perfect and pleasing will for your life.

> And we know that all things work together for good to those who love God, to those who are the called according to His purpose (Romans 8:28).

Now that you see it this way, let's look at a few more things about chaos and how it relates to our destiny.

There are a few truths about chaos; one is that you've got to play by the rules. When you are thrown into a situation where you are forced to play on someone else's playing field, your enemy will often change the rules on you, making it nearly impossible to win in the natural. It's like playing basketball without the home-court advantage. The refs know the other players and their family members well. They overlook a few common—yet easily noticed—fouls from their team, yet when your team performs the most minor infraction, you get fouled. We've all been there, and that is what Satan wants. He wants to place your game on his court with his rules, and while you're there, he will change the rules as he sees fit.

In the natural, if you are fighting a battle with the enemy, don't assume that the rules won't change; you have to be flexible with life and be looking for how the enemy will try to work against you. You have to get good at playing by the enemy's rules in order to develop your game-playing strategies. When we are walking through chaos, things are unpredictable, yet God remains predictable.

Destiny isn't a mystery hidden to never find; it's a blueprint for our lives. Destiny is attainable—something that can be followed through.

In life, God's parameters (rules) are already set. In fact, they were carved in stone back in Moses' day many moons ago. When we try to change the rules and make it our way instead of His, it doesn't work. The rules that we live by are found in God's Word, and getting to know how the rules work will help us understand God's blueprint—or playbook—for our lives. Foundationally speaking, I think one reason some people completely miss their destiny in life is because they don't spend enough time in God's Word. To have presence without parameters (meditating and studying God's Word) means to grow in shallow water. Experiences can come and go, but God's Word remains forever. In this book, I want you to understand that destiny isn't just something that falls in our laps, nor is it something that just happens because we were at the right place at the right time. No, destiny happens in a progressive state because our lives are constantly changing. Better yet, destiny happens in a state of "chaos" or change. This is why it's so important to be rooted in the Word of God—it is the one constant that can guide us more than anything else. As Christians, if we can learn how to read the Bible and apply it to our lives, it would change the entire course of our steps. Learning how to apply the Bible to our everyday lives will help accelerate our destiny. Understanding God's role in the formation of time, creation, and the final days of the supreme reign on earth will help us understand God's role in our lives. This will only come through spending time—precious time—in the Word of God.

Destiny isn't something stumbled upon; it is orchestrated by the divine hand of God.

Destiny isn't something stumbled upon; it is orchestrated by the divine hand of God. God's divine intervention can be revealed at many different stages in our lives. For example, the way I went into that hotel room years ago wasn't the way I left the hotel room. Between the entering and exiting, I had an encounter with God that changed the course of my life. That one moment changed everything about me. God gave me the assurance that He was completely in control, and I chose to follow Him the best way I could. This was a divine moment in my life and I knew I had to act on it. When God gives us divine opportunities and visitations, we have to act. We must move on what He is wanting us to do and when.

Chapter 2: Destiny: What on Earth Is It?

T here are many topics floating around the Internet these days. At random, you could search something different every day of your life and still not discover everything that people are now searching, researching, and teaching. The knowledge that lies at our fingertips is way more than King Solomon or David ever had access to in their entire life. We can tap into it 24/7. Whatever you want to know, you can search and find online. The Bible tells us that the "the era of knowledge" that we live in would be here one day.

> But you, Daniel, shut up the words, and seal the book until the time of the end; many shall run to and fro, and knowledge shall increase (Daniel 12:4).

Yes, knowledge will increase—and it definitely has. But not all knowledge is good. For instance, with the increase of technology, we are also seeing an increase of evil on the earth. That doesn't mean that *all* technology is bad; I am suggesting that *some* of it is. Technology, or power, given over to the wrong hands can be really bad.

Why are so many people searching for so much these days?

Oftentimes, it's because they are empty, walking through life without having any meaning because they lack the fullness of the love of Christ dwelling deep within them. Someone can be filled with all the information they could possibly want, but it won't satisfy like what God can offer to them, which is the unyielding love from our amazing Father. For example, you can be filled with all the information in the world, but you will still remain void and empty on the inside without God's Spirit plugging in the hole. When we allow God to fill us with His love, we allowed Him to completely take over the inner-transformation process within us. Destiny begins when our control ends. Losing control is tough; let's face it—it can be really scary. We all like to be in control, and to reach adulthood you have to make decisions and have some sort of control of your life. But when it comes to our destiny, if we are in control, then God is not. If He is not, then our destiny won't be either. The hardest part of life is letting go; when we let go, He begins. God is in the middle of our letting go. He is right in the center of our ending (giving up). Sometimes God needs us to bring our "stuff" (our control) to an end so He can pick up the pieces.

Time to Take the Plunge

Destiny is like plunging into a river that you've never been in before. It doesn't matter if you know how deep it is, how wide, or what the temperature might be. Prior research about the river might even tell you about what animal and plant life exists in and around it. But the fact is, you've never been in this river. You don't exactly know what you're getting into once you dive in. This is where so many miss it when it relates to knowledge and their destiny. We can study life topics all we want, but if we don't have God's divine intervention in our lives, the end result will be meaningless.

Think about all that some people have accomplished without God's help or blessing. Now pause for a moment and think about what could have been created if those people also had the blessings of the Father in addition to what they established. If God is for you and never against you, then don't you think He wants the best for you in everything that you work on and establish? Yes! He does. He wants the best for you, His child. You're a child of the king, an ancestor of glory, and you deserve His best for your life.

42

We are established in the winds of His mighty breath, forged through the heart of a compassionate Father. He is the designer of life. When we see and believe this, we can experience it in the fullness of Christ. This allows destiny to overwrite all of our shortcomings and weaknesses. It's time to jump! Plan hard and prepare, but jump. So many people miss the "jump" when it's time. Is it scary? Yes. Being scared comes with the territory, and it is part of the whole process. But in the end, God comes through. We may not ever completely understand how He comes through, but He does it. He's there for you—He was right there by your side all along, walking with you through the hard times in life that you needed the most help with. He *was* there, He *is* there, and He *will always* be there. His love never fades and His guidance will never fall short for our lives.

> # Destiny isn't walking in perfection; it's walking, tripping, fumbling around— but trying with a whole heart while holding the hand of God.

Destiny isn't walking in perfection; it's walking, tripping, fumbling around—but trying with a whole heart while holding the hand of God.

God's not looking for perfect people. He is looking for flawed individuals who are willing to say, "God, I can't do this on my own. I need You." When you turn your heart toward Him in this manner, you will touch the heart of God.

43

CHAPTER 3: A LOTTERY TICKET WON'T GET YOU THERE

When some people think of the word *destiny*, they think of "happenstance" or "good fortune." It's like they assume that if they scratch the right circles off a lottery ticket or throw the right numbers at the casino table, life will forever become better and all their worries will eventually go away. That may sound great, but it's not good at all. God never called us to happenstance; He's called us into something much higher than that. God is calling us into destiny through relationship. When we don't have relationship with the Father, we turn toward happenstance, a lottery ticket.

That is why so many people engage in chance-making things like gambling. A quick Internet search will reveal that over 80% of American adults gamble every year. What are they doing? They're trying to get a better life through good fortune or the luck of the dice. They're hoping it will change their life for good. Unfortunately, life doesn't work that way. One after the next they get caught putting another dollar in the slots, or laying another hundred-dollar bill on the table, completely wasting everything they once had earned. What are they wasting? Their hard-earned money! Income that was supposed to pay bills is now the property of the casino owners. The gambler is just chasing fantasies, and now they are walking out of the casino doors with empty pockets. They go home to their spouse and kids ashamed, with a last-ditch plan to work another week so they can take their earnings back to the same casino to "hit it big" next time around.

This story is all too familiar to some. Maybe it's a nightmare to some of you reading this because it's the reality you live in. Maybe a spouse or a loved one is so entrenched with gambling that they can't be trusted with money at all anymore. Satan uses things like this to rob people from their destiny. He loves watching casinos grow and grow and grow—if casinos are growing, then the families and communities built around them are struggling. But the *good news* is that God is in the restoration business!

This chapter isn't about the problems of gambling, but it is about something similar. Gambling may bring quick money and temporary happiness, but unmanaged money made through corrupt means will eventually fade. Take a look at one sobering truth about gambling—a false means of altering our destiny: about a third of lottery winners eventually declare bankruptcy.

Your destiny is never left to chance. Instead, a person's destiny is always found in the hands of our Creator.

How is that so? Because money that is gained quickly is not handled properly. Have you ever seen someone inherit a large amount of money and within a five-year span it's almost all gone, and their lifestyle is once again similar to what it was before the inheritance? I've seen it before. I've seen the power of quick money go through one hand and into another. This is why so many people who leave their lives open to chance end up disappointed—or broke! This is Satan's plan for your life. He wants you to end up empty. So I want to make sure that before we go any further, you and I understand that our lives are not a gamble. This is because your Father in heaven loves you way too much to ever leave anything in your life to chance.

Destiny isn't discovered through something like happenstance, or like a winning lottery ticket. Your destiny is never left to chance. Instead, a person's destiny is always found in the hands of our Creator. There's nothing more important to God than for Him to see your life blossom into what He originally designed for you to become. There's nothing more fervent than the passion that God carries for you. He is always with you and never against you. His thoughts are always toward you and for you. God's arms are never too short for you. He, a loving Father, would never leave your life wide open to chance.

What Destiny Is NOT

Throughout this book you will discover all kinds of different statements and truths about destiny and how it will relate to your life. But before we go deeper in discovering the power of destiny and how it will change your life, lets discuss what destiny is not. Understanding the "nots" will help you grab ahold of the truth about what real destiny is and how it can apply to your life.

1. Destiny Is Not Connected to Fear

I remember a time in my life when fear had gripped me. Fear grabbed me with full force, wrapping its nasty fingers and arms around me, choking me out, one slow move at a time, like a slithering snake coiling around its victim, inching forward to wrap tighter and tighter around its prey. The snake chokes it out, slowly and surely—and before long, it is gone. No turning back. Satan wants the same for me and for you. This is the voice of fear. If we are not careful, we can begin to listen to fear more than faith. When fear walks in, faith heads out the door. This is what fear wants. It wants to force faith out of our life, leaving us to cower and hide behind the closed doors of our homes, not stepping out into our destiny. Look at what the Bible says about fear and how it strips your desire to even want to function in life.

> Fear not, for I am with you; be not dismayed, for I am your God. I will strengthen you, yes, I will help you, I will uphold you with My righteous right hand. (Isaiah 41:10)

47

Destiny won't sit at the table with fear. The two don't get along. Ever!

Satan's grip of fear works around the clock, trying to stop God's children from living in power and presence with God. The Bible tells us that God's perfect love will not mix with our fears.

> There is no fear in love; but perfect love casts out fear, because fear involves torment. But he who fears has not been made perfect in love (1 John 4:18).

Fear will never sit at the table with faith. Love is always the antidote to curing fear.

When we embrace the Father's love, we take on the image of the Father, which is perfect love. Once this happens, it's as if we throw off the old rags and dirty clothes and then the Father places His new clothing on us, unstained and untainted by the world. With the clothing from the Father we have His authority, love, and compassion that shield us from all of the world's wicked ways. This is the fullness of Christ. This is how our fear will turn into faith. God wants the best for us; He wants His perfect will for you. His divine intervention is fighting for you because destiny is called to reign over your life. Allow His love to pour over you, drenching you with inner healing and peace. This is the voice of destiny for your life. Fear will never sit at the table with faith. Love is always the antidote to curing fear.

2. Destiny Doesn't Live with Shame

> But Jesus went to the Mount of Olives. Now early in the morning He came again into the temple, and all the people came to Him; and He sat down and taught them. Then the scribes and Pharisees brought to Him a woman caught in adultery. And when they had set her

48

in the midst, they said to Him, "Teacher, this woman was caught in adultery, in the very act. Now Moses, in the law, commanded us that such should be stoned. But what do You say?" This they said, testing Him, that they might have *something* of which to accuse Him. But Jesus stooped down and wrote on the ground with *His* finger, as though He did not hear. So when they continued asking Him, He raised Himself up and said to them, "He who is without sin among you, let him throw a stone at her first." And again He stooped down and wrote on the ground. Then those who heard *it,* being convicted by *their* conscience, went out one by one, beginning with the oldest *even* to the last. And Jesus was left alone, and the woman standing in the midst. When Jesus had raised Himself up and saw no one but the woman, He said to her, "Woman, where are those accusers of yours? Has no one condemned you?" She said, "No one, Lord." And Jesus said to her, "Neither do I condemn you; go and sin no more." (John 8:1–11)

Look at how Jesus handled this. Did He condemn her? No. Those religious leaders wanted to shame this woman. *Shame*: the five-letter word that everyone wants to erase. Can you imagine the fright on her face, the shame in her heart at that moment? Nobody wants to be humiliated, especially in front of people who are just as guilty. When this woman was brought before Jesus, it was as if the whole world was watching. And in her case, she wasn't the only guilty party present that day. There is a reason why Jesus started writing in the sand, and there is a big reason why all of her accusers eventually left. Those who are guilty of hidden sin and don't handle it properly will attack others around them. This is evidence that they were really functioning out of a religious spirit. That spirit will make sure everyone around them is held to the letter of the law, but it's okay if they break the law themselves.

This is what happened that day. When they all left, what did Jesus do? He looked down at her with compassion and asked, "Where are your accusers?" What a powerful statement wrapped up within a question. Notice the parallel here. In the garden of Eden, Satan asked, "Did God really say that you couldn't eat the fruit?" With one question—the first question in the Bible—mankind bit the fruit, and death entered into the world. Now fast forward to Jesus and the woman in the story above. With one question, Jesus sets a bound, shameful woman free. "Where are your accusers?" I can imagine her looking down at the ground, her body trembling in fear, with tears mingled with sweat trickling down her cheeks; wondering what was this man standing in front of her was going to do next. She carefully peeks around and discovers that all of those who had dragged her to this spot have left. They're all gone, except Jesus! Satan's question killed; Jesus's questions will heal, restore, and bring life. When nobody else is standing next to you, Jesus will still be right there by your side. That is the voice of destiny speaking over you today. It will always heal, always restore, and always speak life over you.

Next Jesus tells her to "Go and sin no more." She didn't have to pay to walk away, write out all of her sins in the sand and then leave, or do any other religious rituals that those other men would have required. Just "leave and stop sinning." That's all He needed to say. Why? Jesus is the voice of destiny. Jesus's voice never caries shame, guilt, or condemnation within it. Jesus has compassion and He is filled with love for all mankind. That includes those who are in very serious and troubling circumstances. He welcomes those to Him who have done the darkest of deeds. Jesus embraces the guilty and welcomes the sinner. That is the voice of destiny speaking over your life. "Go and sin no more! Go and be set free by the Father's love."

3. Destiny Isn't the Voice of Failure

Can you remember a recent failure that happened in your life—a horrible moment in time that you really wish you could just erase so you never have to relive the moment again, even in your mind? These are some of the tough times in life that we all have to go through. Some failures can create a lot of damage in a person's life. Sometimes it can tweak the current condition of how a person lives. When failure comes, it comes to destroy. It comes to bring havoc and stop the person from stepping forward in life. Failure comes from its father, Satan. Failure is a part of a fallen world and it's something that can strike at any time; but God never called us to walk in perpetual failure. He has placed the voice of destiny over our lives. This is a God-given mandate that screams loudly over us. It's a call to succeed in whatever we put our hands to. It's a mandate to try again, and then try again, until we eventually get it right. It's aggressive and not concerned at all with the voice of failure because it knows its source. Destiny doesn't echo the voice of failure; it shouts the voice of victory over your life. Destiny won't have a conversation with disappointment. In fact, if "letdown" sent an email to destiny's inbox, it would go directly to the junk folder.

> # Destiny doesn't echo the voice of failure; it shouts the voice of victory over your life.

When we listen to failure, it will try to cut our future short. Failure breeds hesitation. Destiny produces confidence. God wants us to step out in confident faith. He wants us to live in His presence where there is perfect peace. Failure can't reside where peace is found. When Christ is at the center, peace will be laced throughout our thoughts and actions. Failure has no place in the kingdom—and it certainly doesn't have a place in your mind.

4. Destiny Will Wrestle for Your Future

Destiny can use your past failures and experiences much better than you can. Destiny actually chooses to use your past as a stepping stone for overcoming circumstances. It's been said before, but worth echoing right here: If something in your life has tried to kill you, that is the very thing that God will use to launch you.

When it comes to the past—your past—destiny will use it the way it sees fit. Have you ever watched a wrestling match? Two people are fighting it out in the floor or in a ring. Many times, one tries to overpower the other, when suddenly the situation gets flipped. This is how I would like you to envision your past, especially the moments of failure. Satan will constantly throw your past failures into your future. He does this to try to destroy what God is doing in your life. But God already knows this, so He will overthrow Satan's evil plan and stop Him from destroying what is good in your life. Destiny wrestles for you and chooses to allow what will enter your future from your past. Destiny has the ability to cut off the pain and suffering from your past. This is destiny dreaming for you!

5. Destiny Doesn't Mislead You

Have you ever gone down a long path with someone or something in life only to later discover that you were completely misled? You were tricked, or worse, lied to. Maybe you had a few subtle warnings along the way, or you were given several warning signs but you chose to ignore them. We've all been there, and some of you are at that point right now. Nobody likes to be lied to or made the fool. In this digital age that we live in, sin greatly abounds. There are so many evil tricks out there in the world today. We have to watch our bank accounts, our streets, and who communicates with us on our phones. We have to be vigilant with e-mails and social media, not to mention that we also have to watch over our children and loved ones. We have to stay on top of things practically by the minute now.

When someone watches over you, they are willingly protecting you from an enemy's dangerous tricks. The Lord's tender loving care is always there for you. He is willing to help you at all times and He will never mislead you. He watches over you now and He will be watching over you in the future. Destiny dreams for you in such a way that it has you completely covered by the grace of God. Nothing can penetrate the blood of Jesus. This is destiny for your life. Destiny watches over your life like an owl in the darkness of night. Destiny monitors your life during the day like an eagle soaring in the skies above that can see for miles from his high vantage point. Destiny loves you and will encompass you on all sides of your life. Destiny is the voice, power, and love of God breathing over your life in this very moment while watching over your future—even decades away. Destiny will never mislead you.

> # Destiny is the voice, power, and love of God breathing over your life in this very moment while watching over your future—even decades away

There are many things that can be shared here about what destiny is *not*. We can go on and on with more topics and lists, but the ones in this chapter cover the main areas that most people will struggle with. Satan wants to get you to stop so you won't ever take a step forward ever again. God wants to move you into your dream, the fullness of your destiny. He wants to take the greatest scenario that you can ever think of for your life and get you there. He wants to help you achieve the divine destiny for your life and future. Through the process, we have to be keen to what the Spirit is really saying to us. We have to remain in the Word of God and be able to clearly listen to His still, small voice. It is the voice of the Father that leads you. There are so many voices out there these days speaking at us, trying to convince us that we are not who we really are to get us to shipwreck our lives by turning directions we should not be going. These distractions want us to fail and be miserable instead of walking in the loving presence of our gracious Father. This is why it's so important for a person to learn to hear the Father's voice for themselves. This is what we will discuss in the next chapter.

CHAPTER 4: LED BY THE SPIRIT OR MISLED BY BLIND FATE

B efore we dive into this chapter, I want to make sure that we are on the same page with something very important. There are a lot of ways God will choose to speak to His people—you and me. He can talk to us through His Bible, the Word. He can speak through dreams. He can choose to speak to us through a natural occurrence, like when you lose a job and you recognize that that specific job assignment is now finished. Sometimes God will speak to us through talking with people throughout the day; you are having a normal conversation, but soon you realize that they are speaking directly into your life out of God's divine direction. For me, God speaks to me a lot through dreams at night. So I foster this. I pay close attention to what God is trying to say in my dreams.

This can work the same way for you. Maybe He speaks to you in other ways; the key is that you need to consistently create opportunities for God to speak to you. For example, if you notice that God speaks to you a lot while you're reading your Bible, then guess what you should do? Read your Bible and expect God to speak to you during that time. Have a notebook or something nearby to write down what He says to you.

God speaks to each person in a unique way, so understanding the way He speaks to you is very important. Once you are aware of it, you will notice that He will continue to speak to you in that manner, especially when He knows that you're starting to catch on. So if God spoke to you a certain way once, is that the pattern He is trying to help you follow or is it a one-time occurrence, He spoke to you that way once but He won't speak the same way again? Walking in the Spirit requires us to learn how to consistently hear and follow His voice. The key word is *consistently*. Let's take a look at an example.

How Does "Being Led by the Spirit" Actually Work?

> To them God willed to make known what are the riches of
> the glory of this mystery among the Gentiles: which is Christ
> in you, the hope of glory. (Colossians 1:27)

This is a key scripture about being led by the Spirit of God. Being "led by the Spirit" means that our inner-witness is listening to the Holy Spirit's guidance. That is how God chooses to speak and work through us. Learning to hear God's voice means that we listen carefully to understand what He is asking, and then we are obedient to do what He said to do. Without this principle operating in your life, you won't be able to walk into your destiny. This is one of the higher levels of true relationship. When God's Spirit speaks and you heed the call, it pleases the Father so much so that He will pour out a mighty blessing on your life just for being obedient. Better yet, just for being His!

Being "led by the Spirit" means that our inner-witness is listening to the Holy Spirit's guidance.

Have you ever wondered why God gave so many commands in the Bible? God gives commands to His children in order to bless them. Commands help guide our lives to keep us away from unnecessary trouble. They're not intended to restrict us from living a full and enjoyable life. Instead, God's instructions are designed to prevent us from being harmed.

Decisions, Decisions!

We all have to make decisions every single day of our lives. We've made exceptional ones—the kind of decisions that we look back on and celebrate the moment. Then there are the bad choices that we all make as well. Sometimes we reminisce about the poor decisions we've made in our past. Those are the choices that we tend to regret and could come back to haunt us. There are times when we as individuals aren't the ones making wrong choices, but governments and corporations make choices that we have little or no control over. The entertainment industry has made a fortune on other people's failures. Just look how many blooper and comedy shows are on TV that focus only on showcasing people making stupid decisions. There is an endless supply of online videos available for your laughing leisure. But entertainment industry leaders don't always make great decisions, either.

For instance, in 1982 a popular film producer offered a big-name candy company a scene in his movie featuring their famous candy. The company turned down the offer and the candy scene was replaced with a competitor candy company. In the first month the movie was released, sales for the competitor company skyrocketed. The scene where a shy, lovable alien is lured out of his hiding place with candy is still a classic today. The company that declined the offer probably regrets their decision to this day! These types of decisions are never forgotten, regardless of who makes them.

Let's face some facts here for a moment. We all make horrible mistakes sometimes, and God is aware of it. Yes! That's right. God knows that you are about to make a bad decision and He has a plan already in place to guide you through the repercussions. Every decision we make in life is either led by the Spirit of God or it's directed by humanistic forces on earth. It's been said before, but it's worth saying again: The mind is one of the biggest battlegrounds on earth. Whether it's true or not, I don't know. I can tell you that Satan wants nothing more than to gain control over your mind and your ability to make rational decisions.

Learning how to make important decisions in life is crucial to the outcome of one's destiny. How we choose to live our lives will determine if we fulfill what God has called us to do. That is what I want to discuss with you next.

57

Walking in the Spirit

When it comes to the phrase *walking in the Spirit*, a few faces come to mind. Smith Wigglesworth, for example, is probably one of the most recognized individuals of the twentieth century. The guy had a habit of scaring the religion right out of people. For starters, it has been said that he punched more than one stomach while at the altar praying for people. This would make you think twice before standing in one of Smith's healing lines!

There have been many people who reported that when Smith prayed over them, miraculous things happened. Many people with cancer had the diseased tissue literally fall right out of their body. Some even kept it in a jar to remember what God had done for them and as proof to show to other people that God healed them and could do miracles for them too.

This type of miracle-working lifestyle would be considered crazy to the outsider. Someone coming in off the street into a service where people are holding up jars with a mass of cancer-ridden tissue that used to be inside of someone's body could either scare the daylights out of someone, or it might cause them to see how awesome God really is. For many people, seeing something like this would probably be one of the most remarkable moments of their entire life. This is just one extremely wild example of walking in the Spirit. But with the Father's heart leaning toward you, wild can be common ground with God.

> # Walking with the mind of Christ (being led by the Spirit of God) will never lead you down the wrong path.

Walking with the mind of Christ (being led by the Spirit of God) will never lead you down the wrong path. What might appear to be a bad choice at the moment or to others, if it is led by the Spirit, will always eventually point to a loving God who is holding your hand each step of

· the way. This is the God we serve—He loves you that much! He wants the best for you and His heart is always toward you.

Walking in the Spirit takes time and much attention to learn how to hear the voice of the Father. It also takes a lot of practice. You will make mistakes with this along the way; it comes with the territory, so just keep trying and you'll get it. Sometimes it isn't the Father. Instead, it is our own desires, thoughts, or emotions clouding out what God is saying. That is why it's so important to learn how to read and study the Word of God for yourself. That doesn't mean that we don't go to church or that we're not connected to the body of Christ. In fact, quite the opposite will happen if we draw closer to God. God doesn't want individuals roaming around aimlessly in life by themselves. That is not the heart of the Father for His children. He wants His sheep within His fold, walking, learning, and leaning on Him every moment of every day. That requires relationships! Relationships with God's people will grow stronger as our relationship with the Lord increases. Think about it for a moment: where would you be without the body of Christ in your life? When we draw near to God, He will draw near to us. In the meantime, He gives the church as a gift to be a blessing for our lives. That is the destiny for your life—relationship with the Father and with His church. If this is central to everything you do in life, the result will be marvelous. The outcome will be that you will learn how to walk in the Spirit by the Lord's leading.

God's Sovereignty Is Meant to Bless YOU

Let's take a look at an often misunderstood scripture from the Old Testament. This passage is about mold growing in the walls of homes. It's found in Leviticus.

> Now if the plague comes back and breaks out in the house, after he has taken away the stones, after he has scraped the house, and after it is plastered, then the priest shall come and look; and indeed if the plague has spread in the house, it is an active leprosy in the house.

It is unclean. And he shall break down the house, its
stones, its timber, and all the plaster of the house, and
he shall carry them outside the city to an unclean place
(Leviticus 14:43–45).

What? You have discovered mold growing in your walls more than
once in your house, so now you have to destroy your home completely
and take it to the city dump? Whoa! This really sounds way out there,
doesn't it? This is what a Holy God is all about? He wants you to take
your house, your blessing, and destroy it all because of some lousy
mold? This sure sounds like what is happening if you read this word-
for-word and without any context. When you see the scripture above,
that's what you will tend to think. However, there's something more
to this text worth noting. There's something really important here that
I would like to point out.

Back in this time period, the Israelites were going in and taking
territory (homes and property) from pagan and heathen nations. These
once-powerful nations would create all sorts of false gods and idols
out of material from the land. To protect some of their false gods, the
people would often place their gods inside the walls of the homes.
Sometimes while the foundation was being built, some of the pagan
people would take gods (or idols) and place them into the walls or
under the floor, hoping that that specific god would bless their home
and family. So the Israelites would come in and destroy the pagan
nations and then take over their homes.

Because the children of Israel didn't know if there were idols or
pagan gods inside of the walls or foundation of their homes, God
would allow mold and mildew to start to surface over the areas where
those idols were hidden within their walls or in the ground below the
property. The priest would have to go through a process to determine
if it was normal mold growing or if it was because there were idols
that needed to come out. If things got worse and it kept coming back
after treating it like normal mold being removed, then God would tell
them to tear it all down from top to bottom and start over again. Doing

this would often reveal that there were all kinds of false gods and idols hidden within the walls of the property and dirt below. During this time period, those hidden idols and gods would bring a curse to the house and the land, so this is why God said to get rid of it all—it was contaminated because it was dedicated to false gods.

So now you can see that God wasn't doing this to punish His people—He was working miracles to purge and cleanse the land from pagan things the Israelites couldn't see or detect. Remember, they had recently come out of Egypt, which was one of the false-god capitals of the world. To make matters worse, they had all kinds of false gods around them as they worked and lived right in the region of Egypt's territories. Even though they were a "new generation," they were still just coming out of over four hundred years of slavery. Many of those people would have been used to having those types of things around them, and some may not have been able to detect the evil without the help of a loving and protective God. That is how God works: He creates perimeters, procedures, and guidelines to protect and bless us, not to stop us from having fun or from blessings. That is why God sets parameters for us, to protect us, not to punish us. Think of how many doors closed in our lives over the years. They weren't closing to cause us grief; rather, they closed to stop us from getting hurt down the road. That is the Father's destiny dreaming for you. He is leading you into a divine relationship with Him!

> God creates perimeters, procedures, and guidelines to protect and bless us, not to stop us from having fun or from blessings.

When we walk in the Spirit, we must learn to apply the context of what God is saying to our lives. Having *context* applied to our lives is vital. It is very important to learn to understand how the Lord speaks to you as an individual and within the content of His

Holy Word. As we already discussed, God will never lead you down the wrong path. He will always lead you into divine destiny surrounded by His perfect timing. God doesn't make mistakes about your future.

The voice of destiny is found through the heart of the Father. When we hear His voice, we instantly connect with destiny. When we step forward by listening to His voice and decide to do what God asked us to do, it creates an explosion in the atmosphere. This explosion is God supernaturally falling in love with us!

God's timing and destiny for your life is never ahead of your time—you are always right on time. Destiny doesn't have a time clock; it runs solely off of God's divine plan. It is the Lord's desire for us to learn to follow destiny from increasing glory to increasing glory. That is how destiny works and leads your life. We don't set the time for supernatural manifestations. God handles all of that as we learn to walk by faith. That is why it is so important to learn to be in His presence, being nurtured by the Father. This helps us hear the voice of the Lord calling, the voice of destiny speaking. As much as I would like to stay on this topic for a while, it is also important to know how Satan entangles people in order to mislead them. This is what I want to talk about next.

Blind Fate

Fate is like destiny. Destiny will never mislead you. Some people, however, get caught up in the idea of "blind fate." If you are walking in blind fate, you believe that the things of this world will bring you happiness instead of putting your faith and trust in God alone. My wife's experience is a perfect example of blind fate versus destiny. She had a choice when her former husband passed away at an early age from cancer. She could have either followed blind fate or put her trust in God for her future. Here is what she says about blind fate and destiny:

> I never blamed God for my husband's sickness or death. My life was turned upside down in an instant.

I always knew in my heart that God would take care of me and my kids. I believed He had a plan for my future. During the two years when my husband was sick, I went on a trust walk with Jesus and it changed my life forever. As time went by, I started to think about rebuilding my life again and filling a lonely void after my husband passed away. I wanted someone to take care of me, someone to love again. I began to wonder how this would happen. I only went to work and church, so how would I meet anyone? My trust relationship with my heavenly Father led me to believe I would meet someone supernaturally—God would bring someone to me. I would not seek anyone out. It was very important to me for this person to have the same beliefs as me. God was speaking to me through dreams and visions, and I needed someone who could relate to these experiences. So I rested and waited. However, waiting on God and His timing can be difficult at times. I will admit there were moments when I was tempted to do things on my own. Those Christian dating websites were constantly in my face. What would it hurt? I was so tempted. I believe if I went ahead and tried meeting someone through these sites on my own, I would have missed my destiny and God's plan for my life. My "fate" or destiny would have been blinded by a worldly power. This is where the enemy could have stepped in to counterfeit my blessing. I'm not saying that these sites are bad; I'm saying that I knew that for me, this is not what God wanted for my life. I had to completely trust in Him, not things of this world, for me to walk into what God has called me to. Thankfully, I stayed in faith with what I believed in my heart. He restored what was lost to me—and it was so much more than I could ever have imagined! I now have an amazing husband who I can walk into my destiny with, and my children are loved and cared for beyond measure. His ways are higher than our ways. God is so good!

This goes to show you how easy the world may lure you into "blind fate" instead of seeking out God's plan for your life. Imagine if my wife had not listened to her heart when God said wait and be still. If she went ahead of God's timing, she may not have found the path which will lead her into her destiny.

Blind Fate and the Entitlement Mentality

Blind fate comes from a world view that says, "I have to have it. I'm entitled to it. I can do anything." All of these statements are false, and they stem from a distorted view of who God really is and how He functions with His people. Blind fate is a delusion that entraps a person to a point where it becomes too late to fix the mess that they are now in. This transpires because the individual gets sidetracked from the original calling that was placed on their lives. Let's take a look at these three areas of blind fate:

> Blind fate is a delusion that entraps a person to a point where it becomes too late to fix the mess that they are now in.

"I Have to Have It"

This is what the world teaches us. This is where we take some of our first steps toward greed. *Greed* refers to having an excessive, selfish desire to have more of something than you need (like money, possessions, or food).

Did you get that? Greed is a desire to have something that we should not have at all. Greed is rampant in our day and age, and a lot of it runs right through all of the media outlets that we watch. Through social media, online videos, TV commercials, and so on, the world says "You have to have this." All of these venues try to get you to believe that you are not important unless you have something that other people have. In fact, it's normally something that you really shouldn't have or don't need. That is how society builds social status in a country or person's life. If you don't have it, you're not really important. So people go out and get all the latest fads and styles, only to rack up more and more credit card debt. Once the cards are maxed out, your destiny lies in shambles because you can't move forward even if you wanted to. You now have to go back and erase all of the bad debt you built up from "keeping up with the Joneses" (or should I say the Kardashians).

If your self-worth is based on what you have, you're going to live a very miserable life. Every day, credit card companies, banks, mortgage lenders, advertisement and marketing firms, and massive media companies team up to offer you a better life by trying to convince you to keep up some of the most powerful, influential, and wealthiest people on the earth. This isn't the heart of the Father toward you because this type of blind fate will only leave you high and dry, desperate and wanting more. The voice of the Father always leads you to the fullness of Christ.

"I'm Entitled to Have That"

Another area of blind fate is the idea that you are entitled to have something.

Once again, this idea is running rampant in our society today. In some regions of the Unites States, the entire culture and mentality of that area is based on this idea, which is nothing more than a delusion. This "curse" in our society is growing like a weed and it's starting to become accepted as fact among some of our younger generations.

This idea teaches that if someone else has something that you want, you rightfully should have it too because you're just as good or better than that person is. In other words, what is theirs is rightfully yours. People who play this card and game will normally use their upbringing or heritage to attempt to rob others blind.

> # The entitlement mentality is like a cancer to a person's destiny.

It doesn't matter where your ancestors came from or went through; the fact is that they are gone and you can't go back to change it—good or bad. In addition to this, if someone wronged your ancestors, it doesn't mean that someone now owes you something. The bottom line is that all of us have been wronged before. We have all gone through things in life that we can't stand to remember or ever bring up again. This doesn't give us the right to "take" from other people. The entitlement mentality is like a cancer to a person's destiny. It will cause someone to live in an apathetic state of mind (Lack of feeling, motivation, or interest). It will cause someone to wander aimlessly from place to place, always chasing fantasies and never obtaining all that God has set before them. This is not the voice of destiny speaking for you. It's the voice of defeat lying to you.

What other people worked hard for is theirs. It's their right to have and enjoy. We often look at what our parents or older people have enjoyed over the years and we immediately want what they have, but better. This is entitlement. What it doesn't teach you is the fact that the previous generation had to work really hard to get where they are today, and some of them helped lay a better foundation for your life. That is what we must be thankful for. That is why we are to honor our elders.

"I Can Do Anything That I Want in Life"

The other lie that the world likes to teach us is that we can do anything that we want to do in life. This sounds great—it really does. I would guess that this message has been mixed with blind faith too many times behind our church pulpits. Most preachers have probably even said something like it before. The idea is that whatever we put our minds to, we can do. It sounds awesome; inspiring, to say the least. And with faith, all things are definitely possible, right? *Wrong!*

The world wants you to believe that you can become something that you're not—something you were never designed to be. Media pumps this idea out into the airwaves all the time and they welcome the idea of you grasping hold of this concept. They want you to chase a fantasy that isn't yours to chase or have. The fact is, we can set new records all day long, climb new heights all week, and invent things that have never been invented before. We're human, so we can do almost anything. But that's the key word: *almost.* We can accomplish a lot, but outside of the Father's will for our lives, there are some things that we really shouldn't try.

When we attempt to do what God hasn't asked us to do, it only opens doors of disaster over our lives. God has a perfect plan for your life. Sometimes this plan may seem long-term, extremely hard to reach, and on some occasions, impossible. But when we mix in the Father's love, His call for our lives, and then choose to do what He wants us to do, that is where the impossible overtakes the practical. This is how God wants us to live—in the impossible, yet still connected to the natural realm. Let me give you an example.

On Sunday, August 16th, 2009, a runner from Jamaica emerged from the unknown and became the fastest runner in world history—sprinting 100 meters in the record time of 9.58 seconds. This remains the world record, currently set by Jamaican superstar Usain Bolt.

> # When we attempt to do what God hasn't asked us to do, it only opens doors of disaster over our lives.

Without a doubt, this is supernatural—he broke all natural records and it may be a while before someone else steps up to the starting block and delivers something greater than this. My point? There are many details in the mix here that helped Usain arrive at this amazing victory, one being his design. God obviously created Usain to be a runner, and a fast one at that. Secondly, he pushed it, worked it, and stayed with it. We don't know a lot about his upbringing; we do know that he obviously didn't just wake up the morning of the race and decide to set a world record in sprinting. Instead, he worked at it really hard. It's one thing for someone to want to set a world record; it's another thing for them to actually do it. Breaking a world record became part of Usain Bolt's destiny, *but it came through hard work*. At the age of twenty-three, he had to decide to either attempt something that had never been done before and take the risk of failing on world television, or stop what he was training for and do something different, something less risky. What went on behind the scenes to get him there, we may never know. But what we do know is that persistence helped in the matter.

What If Your Identity Has Been Built Upon Delusion?

The three areas above will drive you right into delusion—something that is completely false. God doesn't lead His people into areas that will shipwreck or destroy their lives. That is not His nature. God's nature is based on His loving heart toward you, as His most precious and chosen creation. The delusion comes when we try to reach past the boundaries that the Lord has set for us. When we try to become what God hasn't created us to be, we end up living a lie, a misconception that ensnares our destiny. This explains why so many people are walking around aimlessly right now on earth. Worst yet, too many are walking in and out of the doors of our churches each week—and some are even more delusional than the world!

What we must do, first and foremost, is look into our own lives and see if there are areas where we are not the "real" us. Who are we trying to be, or who are we trying to fool? When it comes to destiny, we might be fooling people around us, but we are not fooling God. When we realize the seriousness of God's perfect will for our lives, we must also realize the importance of fleeing from our own delusions. Not everyone can live in fame and fortune, and there aren't enough international platforms for everybody on earth to stand on. The fact is that someone has to turn the lights on and off, and someone also has to clean up the facilities when everyone is gone. If everyone is a superhero, then really nobody is a superhero. God may be calling you to complete some of the most amazing things ever accomplished on earth, but it won't happen overnight, and it certainly won't happen alone. Living in the supernatural requires a long-term process, and until you are there—where God wants you to be—you must learn how to avoid living in a delusion, something that isn't yours, and never was to begin with. The Lord is gracious and kind to His people and He will do whatever it takes to help you get out of the mess that you might be walking in. He is aware of all of the lies that you attempt to live, and how you put on a mask to hide your true identity. God is there for you and will help you walk these issues out.

Destiny Won't Mislead You

As I mentioned before, Jesus will never mislead you, and destiny won't either. When destiny is speaking to you, it is the voice of God calling you, leading you to become who you are in Christ. When we walk in Christ, we embrace the Lord's fullest potential. So why do so many good people—good Christians—start off on the right foot in life and eventually go way out there in the deep end somewhere? It's like they start the race God gave them, but the end of their life is nothing but one big ball of mess. They made great decisions with good intentions at first, but along the way something went wrong.

The result of being misled can be tragic. For instance, let's take a look at Mark Chapman. Who, you ask? Mark Chapman—don't you remember him? Most don't remember Mark, but they remember who he killed: John Lennon. At forty years old, Mark Chapman shot at John Lennon five times with a Charter Arms .38 handgun. Four of the five bullets hit John Lennon in the back, killing him. Mark claimed that he had shot John Lennon to get attention.

Attention! That's all! Isn't that something? This behavior comes from being led by Satan, which will always lead you to destruction. When we don't hear the voice of the Father's love, it will eventually drive us into a delusional mindset. That isn't how the Father leads us at all. He will never direct us to do anything that is contrary to His nature, which is first and foremost *love*. Doing things like what Mark did will only lead us into blind fate. Once there, blind fate will destroy your life if you allow it. How do we know this? Well, let's break this down here and see exactly what blind fate is.

I'm not here to write about whether or not Mark Chapman is a Christian and/or when did he become a Christian. I want to focus our attention on Mark's actions. Mark, if led by the Spirit, would not have been led to shoot someone in the back in cold blood. In fact, you could put any person in the same situation, and it still doesn't mix with destiny and what God wants for your life. You can insert your worst enemy into the story here, and God would never tell you to kill them.

There are moral and civil laws, of course, and there are military and governmental reasons for why it may be necessary to take a person's life. If you are reading this right now and you have had to take a person's life, it's probably something that you don't want to remember or talk about. The issue here isn't all the reasons why or why not someone can take a life; the issue is that an innocent person was shot in cold blood who had no connection to the killer at all. The reason for John's tragic death was nothing more than the killer wanting to be famous. Well, now he is sitting in prison for life somewhere. Was this destiny for him? No.

Delusion will always bring destruction. That was delusion; it is evil that leads someone to destroy another person's life. That is *not* how destiny works; that is Satan's misleading.

Blind fate is wishful thinking. It is chasing fantasy.

Blind fate is like filling your car up with gas, driving until it runs dry, then hoping that you will meet your new spouse, get a new job, and become a millionaire, all in the same week. Blind fate is wishful thinking. It is chasing fantasy. Proverbs talks to us about this.

Led by the Spirit or Misled by Blind Fate

He who tills his land will be satisfied with bread, but he who follows frivolity *is* devoid of understanding. (Proverbs 12: 11)

A hard worker has plenty of food, but a person who chases fantasies ends up in poverty. (Proverbs 28:19 NLT)

When we chase fantasies, we create a situation that causes us to look into our future in such a way that we miss what God is doing right here, right now.

Walking in destiny won't happen if we carelessly try to discover our destiny on a limb God never asked us to walk out on. Blind fate has us focusing on our personal matters when we should be handling other areas of responsibility like mowing the lawn, working hard at our job, cleaning the house, and feeding and taking care of our kids. Blind fate will trick us into waiting our entire lives for a pro football, basketball, or baseball invitation when we aren't called to go to any of them. Blind fate causes a writer to miss out on what they should be writing down right now because they are hoping someone else will fund the project for them. Blind fate causes us to not be ready, and so when the "boats of destiny" show up at the dock, it's too late. Why? We're not ready—and that's exactly what Satan wanted!

Blind fate will cause us to not be prepared. It will cause us to sit idle when we should be working hard. Hard work is what I learned from my father's contracting business. I am so grateful for it because it has helped me become a more anointed minister. Being diligent is extremely important to hearing our destiny, and it is what I learned from my father. He taught me to be ready, be prepared, work hard, and stay on a task until it's completed. He also taught me to stick with it when no one else would. This life skill is invaluable to me now because it has allowed me to know the difference between destiny speaking to me and blind fate trying to derail me.

71

Blind Fate Will Always Derail You

This is the plan, the goal, the dream, and voice of blind fate: to derail you for life and cause you to miss the boat that won't ever come back. When this happens, it can take a lifetime to fix. Have you ever arrived somewhere only to realize that you don't belong there? This happens all the time in life, and, unfortunately, it happens way too much in the church today. How is it so? Why is blind fate leading Christians just as much as non-believers? The answer is found in the Bible. Let's look at Elijah for a moment.

> And Ahab told Jezebel all that Elijah had done, also how he had executed all the prophets with the sword. Then Jezebel sent a messenger to Elijah, saying, "So let the gods do to me, and more also, if I do not make your life as the life of one of them by tomorrow about this time." And when he saw that, he arose and ran for his life, and went to Beersheba, which belongs to Judah, and left his servant there.
>
> But he himself went a day's journey into the wilderness, and came and sat down under a broom tree. And he prayed that he might die, and said, "It is enough! Now, Lord, take my life, for I am no better than my fathers!"
>
> Then as he lay and slept under a broom tree, suddenly an angel touched him, and said to him, "Arise and eat." (1 Kings 19:1–5)

Elijah was known for operating by the Spirit of the Lord. That means that Elijah consistently acted on the voice of the Lord, but he also moved in God's timing. Knowing when it's time to act on what you have heard God say is vital to learning to hear the voice of the Father. This is so important. If you hear the voice of the Lord—destiny speaking—and you miss the timing of it, you just missed it completely. This is the same as not hearing God on something and moving out on it anyway. Both end in disaster. Disaster is the end result of blind fate. God doesn't intentionally lead His people into disaster.

> # If you hear the voice of the Lord— destiny speaking—and you miss the timing of it, you just missed it completely.

In this instance, Elijah completely missed it. Aren't you glad that God kept the "human" sides of people in the Bible? He didn't delete or erase their weaknesses; rather, He kept them in the Bible for all of us to read about centuries later. Elijah got scared, and he blew it! When Jezebel rose up against Elijah, he took off out of fear. When fear steps in, faith leaves. Think about that for a moment. Elijah just watched all of the false prophets of Baal and Asherah get defeated and slaughtered, yet now he's running away from God's will because of one single person: Jezebel. That doesn't make sense at all, does it?

Sometimes we can become so delusional, so frightened, that we no longer think rationally. It is a dangerous place to be in, and that is where Elijah was. If we were there in that moment, we would have seen the fear written all over his face. Have you ever seen fear in someone's eyes? That is what I'm talking about; that is what Elijah was facing that day. He was scared for his life, so he ran far away. The voice of blind fate will always lead you into delusion and then destruction.

Delusion wants you to think that you are over—it's done, it's all hopeless, and there isn't anything good coming out of your situation. Delusion wants you to believe that you can't find a way out, a way of escape. The result is that it will normally convince you to do things against the will of the Lord. That is what happened to Elijah, and it can happen to anyone. But I love the end result, the final process here. As always, God steps in. It's His gracious intervention that leads us back to the right course in life.

This is also the power of intimacy and having a personal relationship with our Father God. Intimacy is crucial because if Elijah didn't have a deep relationship with God, then He might not have recognized what God was saying to Him to turn back to the correct path. Intimacy with the Father will help us correct the mistakes we made before it's too late.

Later on, the Lord basically told Elijah, "Go back the exact way you came. And while you're at it, Elijah, return to your destiny by anointing Hazael to be the king of Aram and anoint Jehu to be king over Israel." Jehu was the person who later removed Jezebel from power. Then God reminded Elijah that he wasn't alone—God had set aside seven thousand Israelites who were not willing to bow to Baal and the evil ways of Jezebel. That is the Lord I know and serve! That is the power of an unconditional Father loving on His most delightful treasure: YOU!

Destiny doesn't lead us into destruction, but to safe streams and bountiful fields. Destiny speaks to us and leads us into a safe haven of rest and divine discovery. Destiny's language will always be filled with divine peace from the throne of grace. God's still, soft voice will always guide us into a serene place.

CHAPTER 5: YOU ARE NOT AN ACCIDENT

Accidents happen. We've all had and heard of them. Accidents never get our permission, nor do they ever show up at a good time. Most people will tell you that accidents of any kind normally show up at the worst possible time. A calamity is something that occurs that takes us off of our focus. For example, say you're driving to the store or an important appointment and you get caught in traffic, rear-ended, or your tire pops. Nobody got hurt or killed, but it's an inconvenience. Sometimes accidents are fostered by bad decisions, like not listening to the Father's voice.

> ## Sometimes accidents are fostered by bad decisions, like not listening to the Father's voice.

I would like to share with you an accident worth mentioning. It probably sounds worse than what it was, but if it wasn't handled properly by the rescue team, someone, including myself, could have died. This accident was progressive. It was something that could have and should have been avoided. Looking back, the culprit was me; I chose not to listen to the Holy Spirit and decided to take matters in my own hands.

What you're about to read actually happened. I was an eyewitness because I'm the one who led the whole mess.

The Tree, the Lift, and the Near-Accident

This story is going to sound crazy, but I've got to tell you about a really bizarre construction incident that happened to me. It threw me for a loop—and it all could have been avoided if I had followed the voice of the Lord.

It was during a time when business was slowing down, and I really could have used a little more cash. I was in the middle of a job working for an elderly woman when she asked if I knew anyone who could cut a tree down in her yard. I instantly saw dollar signs, and I agreed to take the job for myself without even looking at the tree. There was one problem: the tree was massive, and I had no experience in tree removal. To be honest, I had no business taking or trying this job. As the date approached, I started to have checks in my spirit. I considered hiring a tree-removal specialist to remove the tree. However, greed and pride took over, and I decided to do the job myself.

The day arrived, and I rented an eighty-foot lift. As my worker and I were driving toward the house, fear sank in. Looking back, there were numerous signs trying to stop us from getting into the lift. The first thing was that the lift was supposed to be an eight-hour rental, and they dropped it off two hours late. Now I was running two hours behind schedule and only had six hours to remove this giant tree. Next, we had difficulty changing the saw blade on the chainsaw and lost another hour. After three hours of wasted time, I was excited to finally get into the lift and get started.

We learned how to use the machine by cutting the smaller branches first. Things were going great and I thought I was the man. As the machine got higher and higher, so did my pride and arrogance. This was a piece of cake! Then suddenly the machine stopped working properly. An alarm burst through my pride bubble. The machine started to shut down because we were not on level ground. We repositioned the lift, which helped, but the machine ran slower the rest of the day, hindering our progress even more.

We started cutting branches again and bringing the lift higher and higher. The tree was huge! It was ten feet in diameter at the base, and the lift didn't even reach the top of the tree. As we were working, bringing the lift up and down, back and forth, God spoke to me and said, "Sal, you should bring a rope." I didn't listen. Maybe if I had, it would have prevented the disaster that was about to happen.

As we went up again, we worked on cutting one of the bigger branches off of the tree. Down went the branch. As if in slow motion, I watched it fall to the ground. It was almost to the ground, and bam! The branch landed on the hydraulics, damaging the system and knocking out the power. There we were, just the two of us, completely suspended in the air with a broken lift machine and no way to get down. Of all things, the wind started to pick up as the weather began to shift, and we were stuck! The winds started to move around us, and we were swaying. Time was quickly passing by. We had hoped to be done with the tree-removal project and out of there by then.

A graduation party was going on nearby. We began yelling for someone to call 911. Eventually emergency services arrived and addressed the situation. Yes, the lift was indeed broken, and we were stuck nearly sixty-seven feet up in the air. To top things off, there was no easy way to get to us because of the surrounding trees and where we were positioned. The fire department decided to use their ladder truck to get to us. Well, the ladder truck ended up being too short to reach us. Again, we were suspended sixty-seven feet in the air. I know this because the fire department had to take measurements to make sure they got the right sized ladder truck to rescue us. It seemed like forever before the right truck finally arrived. Because of the winds and where we were located, the ladder truck could only inch along to where our lift was. It was a painstaking process, and finally the ladder stopped three to four feet from our lift. It could not get any closer, but it was close enough to attempt a rescue. I wouldn't say the next step was a Hollywood stunt scene, but it sure felt like it! Getting from our lift to the ladder truck was a scary feat in itself.

What was supposed to take no more than six hours ended up going late into the evening. We both finally made it to the soggy, grassy ground. Wait, did I say soggy?

Eventually the fire department came back around and assessed things further. They later told me that I had placed our heavy lift machine over an underground creek that runs through the area. Remember the alarm going off? That was one sign that I definitely should NOT have ignored! To make matters worse, it turns out that the lift was leaking oil into the river. Do you know what that meant? I had to pay a clean-up service fee. I couldn't believe it! The fire department told me that if I didn't pay the fee immediately, they would contact an environmental agency, which would come after me for an even bigger clean-up service fee. So I paid the fee to the fire department and was happy that it was all over. Or so I thought.

The lift rental company contacted me and told me I caused thousands of dollars of damage to the machine when the huge branch hit it. I've been around construction most of my life and I know a thing or two about construction equipment. I've been around broken machines plenty of times, and I have a good idea what something is going to cost for repairs. What the rental company quoted me wasn't anything near what it should have been to fix the machine—it was a bit excessive. Eventually, my insurance company stepped in, and things were resolved to my favor.

When all was said and done, I had learned a few lessons. For starters, I received more than one warning about this project. I received several, actually, yet I chose to ignore them all. I also realized that from that moment forward I should only take on projects I was qualified for. Tree climbing and removal have nothing to do with the construction business, or at least not in my world. A very important lesson I learned is that when I start to get warning signs from the Lord, I should stop, listen, and pray for direction.

In the end, I hired a tree removal specialist to finish taking down the tree. It cost me more money in the end than if I had just listened to my spirit and hired him in the first place. What a hard lesson to learn!

There was something else I learned that day. God knew that we were stepping out on a limb (literally!). He knew that this was out of our league and was going to be extremely dangerous. In spite of my ignorance in not listening to the Lord, God's love kept us safe—even though I was being disobedient. What could have been a horrible accident, something that could have cost a lot of money in damages, and could have caused harm to my worker, myself, or the rescue team, turned out to be an extremely hard lesson to learn. In my humility, God showed up that day. That is the incredible power of the God we serve.

From the beginning of your life, He has had you right in the palm of His hands. We make mistakes and accidents every day of our lives, but God does not. When He fashioned you, He made no mistake. You were not an accident. You are truly precious in His eyes. Accidents happen in life, but you are not one!

We make mistakes and accidents every day of our lives, but God does not. When He fashioned you, He made no mistake.

In the Womb

Without a doubt, the way a woman's body is made and the process of how they develop to carry life within their womb is remarkably supernatural. Taking this a little further, how a child is born is nothing less than a miracle. When God made woman, He made a being that is extremely delicate and special. If you've ever witnessed a child being born, then you have witnessed a marvelous procedure that is beyond natural comprehension. That is how special God made women. I don't think that they get the credit they deserve sometimes.

Where would we be without the tender love of a mother? God made women to show a side of His love that isn't found in a man's emotional

79

being. They will give their lives to nurture because that is who they are and how God designed them to operate.

Women have an extraordinary ability to display the firmness of the Father, the unconditional love of God, and the grace given through Jesus Christ all in one. Personally, I believe one of the greatest revelations is simply found in how God showed His love and unwavering commitment in creating the woman. This is vital for knowing how to walk in the Spirit. You can't walk in the Spirit if you aren't able to embrace God's unconditional love. The Father's passion toward you was already there, long before you were conceived.

The whole time you're in the womb, you're not just developing physically; you're also developing spiritually.

We know that life begins at conception, but for the Lord, your life started the moment He thought about you. We don't have time to go through all of the stages of a pregnancy and the delivery process; that's not what this is about. But we do have to look at a few key steps of a mother's pregnancy. I want you to see this through the process of you being born and how God meticulously formed you within your mother's womb. I also want you to realize that God was speaking to you while you were in the womb. You may not remember what was going on in the womb, but you were still alive, so God could speak to you at that stage in life. If I could tell you what God was saying to me back then, it would be something like this: "There's Sal. That's my boy! I am so proud of him already. I see destiny all through his life." That is how He was speaking.

So many critical things happened while you were developing inside your mother's womb. At six weeks after conception, you grew to a size of a pea. You started to develop your face, neck, and vital organs. A few months later you began to move around and you could blink your eyes. Your toes and hands were forming. At around twenty-four weeks, you were a little over a pound and you could hear sounds outside of the womb. At the end stage of pregnancy (36-40 weeks), you were growing rapidly. Your brain and lungs were almost fully developed. You were getting ready to emerge into the world.

The whole time you were in the womb, you were not just developing physically; you were also developing spiritually. The breath of life was dropped into you, and you were being formed—fashioned by the hand of God. The Creator of the universe dropped everything else to perfectly craft you. That is how much God cares for you. You're not an accident; you never were an accident! It doesn't matter how you were born or if you know your parents or not. It doesn't even matter if your parents care for you. The fact is that God loves you and deeply cares for you.

> Before I formed you in the womb I knew you; before you were born I sanctified you; I ordained you a prophet to the nations. (Jeremiah 1:5)

The Bible speaks about this loud and clear. It can't be said any better than how Jeremiah puts it. God *loves* you! Some translations, like the one above, literally say, "Before I formed you in the womb, I *knew* you."

God makes no mistakes—and He made none whatsoever when He formed you in your mother's womb. He spoke you into being, and even before you began to form the first and smallest part of your body, God had already placed within you a seed of destiny. This seed is His life-giving DNA for you, and it is only for you and nobody else.

I find it interesting that scientists have proven that babies start to hear the outside world at around twenty-five or twenty-six weeks of pregnancy. According to this one statement, the baby—YOU—can start to hear muffled sounds around you, most importantly from the mother. Sometime before the baby is born, they can even start to "communicate" in their own way to certain voices or common sounds that they begin to pick up. And all along, while we were being fashioned by the hand of our Master, we were learning the Father's love. His tender hands were forming us within a well-nourished womb. It's been said that there is nothing like the love a mother has toward her child. Mothers will do anything to save their children, even if it's giving their life for their child; and yet, God's love for you is much greater than this. When He thought of you, He formed you, and while He was forming you, He also fell in love with you. While you were in the womb, He was teaching you how to hear His voice. What a caring Father!

Out of the Womb

At forty weeks, you're ready to come out of the womb. Contractions begin, and you get into position for delivery. In the most common scenario, the water breaks, and you are ready for exit! All this time you were being molded in the womb by the Creator of the world.

> For You formed my inward parts; You covered me in my mother's womb. I will praise You, for I am fearfully *and* wonderfully made; Marvelous are Your works, And *that* my soul knows very well. (Psalm 139:13–14)

Soon you take your first breath after entering the world outside the womb. It may be the first breath of air, but to the Lord, you're breathing in His breath of life. The whole time you were being fashioned (perfected) in the womb, you couldn't see God, but He was staring right at you; His face was near your face and His eyes were staring into your eyes. You are His treasured possession. To be wanted is one thing, to be welcomed can feel wonderful, but to be both loved and welcomed by the King of Glory is priceless!

Just like you were in the womb, the supernatural protective realm of your mother's stomach, now you are in the supernatural protective realm of the Almighty. With God's love working toward you, His comforting presence cannot be taken away from you—ever!

Growing Pains

There are certain things you can't control in life. You can't control what went on in the womb or when you are born or decisions made by others when you were a child. For me, it was when I was four years old and my parents decided to divorce.

I was raised by a single mom who worked hard to raise two boys. She went to nursing school during the day and worked third shift many endless nights. I saw my dad occasionally, and the more I saw him, the more I wanted to get to know him. At the age of fifteen, I began to work in my father's business part-time, and at seventeen I moved in with him.

Growing up, I had made some bad decisions of my own. I was a reckless teenager who was always finding trouble. These reckless decisions led me to drop out of college, and before long, I was working full-time in the family business. I experimented with drugs in my early teen years, and by the age of twenty I couldn't live without them. Partying became my life. The drugs and alcohol filled a void I couldn't explain. I was spinning out of control.

I thought I had it all figured out. Drugs, pride, arrogance, and the almighty dollar ruled my life. After I had gone into the family business, I believed that I was going to acquire a bunch of rental properties. My goal was to retire at the age of forty as a wealthy man. This is where things went wrong for me. Let's just say that my drug addiction and ridiculous decisions tended to get in the way, and the only thoughts I had were of grandeur and a delusional way of life.

One thing I can say is that my dad trained me well in the construction business. I was especially good at framing doors and windows. There were times, however, when my drug addiction got in the way of my success as a contractor. Once I was so "stoned" that I put the hinges on the same side as the doorknob. What a waste of time and money that was! Looking back, there were many times where I wasted everyone's time and money because of my stupidity. Not only that, I put people's lives at risk with no regard for my own life. I can only imagine what my dad's workers and contractors thought about me, the boss's son.

Luckily for me, I had a dad who loved me, and I'm sure it wasn't always easy. In fact, it was downright frustrating and explosive at times. My dad kept loving me and giving me chance after chance. I went through this difficult period in my life thinking that I had entitlement and a free ride in the family business. I never did achieve my goal to retire at forty. But through the ups and downs along the way, I learned a lot. This learning curve came from both my earthly father and my heavenly Father. My heavenly Father gave me hope. He was patient as I walked through the process of learning who I was in Him. I almost missed my blessing because of my pride and arrogance. I praise God every day that He loves me and found me just in the nick of time. My life changed forever!

A Distorted Version of Your Destiny

Satan wants to cause us to miss out on all that the Father has for us. Satan wants us to miss the Father's blessing. One way blessings will come is through God honoring the work of our hands. He redeems the curse of this earth through the effort that we put forth. This is what I like to call "taking kingdom territory for the Lord." He wants us to prosper in everything we do, and He wants us to take dominion over this earth while we wait for His return one day.

> And the Lord will make you the head and not the tail;
> you shall be above only, and not be beneath, if you
> heed the commandments of the Lord your God, which
> I command you today, and are careful to observe them.
> (Deuteronomy 28:13)

Hard work will always be blessed. God speaks over and over again in the Bible about how dangerous lazy people are. Just look in Proverbs and read what God has to say about lazy people. He makes it very clear that lazy, undedicated people will not be blessed. They will not be prosperous because God cannot consecrate a lazy person. He can't honor a half-hearted individual. It's been said that extremely successful people—those who did extraordinary things in life—all have one

84

specific thing in common. In other words, if you lined all of the world-record breakers, international voices, and famous inventors, they all had one trait that every person who ever studied them would all pick up on. Would you like to take a guess at what the one single commonality of the most successful people in the world is?

All of them spent roughly thousands of hours of hard-earned, dedicated work to become successful. Nobody told them to. Nobody funded them—they did because they saw the passion, the call, and the duty of what they were doing and they refused to stop. They pressed on into the late hours of the night. They pushed and pushed while everyone else was sleeping, and they were awake and going again at the crack of dawn, refusing to stop.

> # When we walk in the Lord's destiny, things will prosper. They will advance for the glory of God.

When we walk in the Lord's destiny, things will prosper. They will advance for the glory of God. This doesn't come through taking it easy or living a half-hearted life. When I was messing up and living a bad life working for my dad, I was wasting God's time as well. Pursuing God's heart is never wasted time; instead, it's devoted time toward Him. His love drives us deep into the wells of His eternal glory. That is what He wants for us, and that is what He wanted for me back in that day. Sadly, I was walking in a distorted view of who God was, which was causing me to feel poorly about myself. If we don't have the correct view of God and the Father's pure love toward us, then we won't have a correct perspective about life or ourselves. That is what happened to me.

When we walk in a distorted view of who God really is, it will cause us to direct our attention to things that aren't pleasing to Him. These behaviors will often drive us into one mess after the next. It's almost like a person decides to walk out into some dangerous waters, and once they are in the rough current, they get swept away. The worst part is that they chose to do it all by themselves. They didn't tell anyone that they were going into the deep and dangerous waters that day. Adding more to the chaos, they chose to not wear the proper protective gear, like footwear that would protect them in the water. And they decided not to wear a life vest or carry any rope or additional supplies that could have helped them in case something happened.

This is an example of one delusional decision after the next. We stop living life for a holy Father, and instead we blame Him when things fall apart, as though it were His fault. Delusion will cause you to get swept away downriver without any help. It's like floating down a polluted creak without a paddle. You're getting nowhere fast and your life is consistently out of control, moving from one disaster to the next. It's like a bad movie getting worse, except you are the star of the film and all of the bad drama is happening to you, with no superhero to sweep you out of the trouble. That is how Satan wants you to live. He wants you to live a delusional life filled with chaos that isn't built around God's truth. It clouds your perspective and causes you to not be able to see the destiny that God has waiting for you.

Delusion Will Create Regret

When we buy into delusion, we are really taking the bait of Satan. We ultimately end up giving in to his well-planned attack that's designed to make us unproductive. The real delusion of it all is that we listen to the lies of the enemy so well that we become convinced that our unproductive life is all for a good cause. He wants us to believe that nothing will ever work out. He wants nothing more than for us to stop and walk away from God's plan and destiny for our lives. He wants us to walk away from all of our battles, never again fighting for what we believe in.

When we submit to delusion, we give up on the heart of the Father for us. We stop dreaming for ourselves because we become convinced that even God has given up on us. This is a dangerous place to be because we start missing God-appointed opportunities. One after the next, over and over again, those God-moments are missed—and some opportunities, once they pass by, will never come back around. Delusional thoughts set in further, going deeper and deeper into the mind and into the soulish nature of who we are. If we aren't careful, we start believing that all is lost and nothing is worth defending anymore.

> # The real delusion of it all is that we listen to the lies of the enemy so well that we become convinced that our unproductive life is all for a good cause.

About this time, regret will soon start moving in. It's one thing to miss a few great opportunities in life, grow from them, and look for better ones down the road. It's another thing to miss out over and over again. Delusion will cause us to miss the mark in life. Delusion will create regret, which saps our hope. That is what Satan wants. He would rather fight an army of people filled with hopelessness than one individual who starts to believe again. In the natural, the most dangerous people on earth are those who have given up all hope; they can cause a lot of damage. In the supernatural, one of the scariest people to Satan is someone who was hopeless and has started to believe again. Go ahead! Take a fresh breath of hope right now! I want you to believe! I want you to grab hold of who you are in Christ and what God can do in your life. This is what it's all about.

HOPE Will Take You from Slavery to Freedom

One of the greatest powers on earth is the ability to hope. It is the sure understanding that God is for you and not against you.

> I can do all things through Christ who strengthens me. (Philippians 4:13)

The power of hope can change the course of a person's life. It's hope that causes people to go above and beyond the call of duty for their lives. Hope breathes deep into the heart of God's child, a voice of destiny calling out for them to succeed. He only has the best set aside for you. He has only the greatest thoughts for you. His blueprint for your life isn't unreachable; it's attainable. God loves you and hopes the best for you.

> ## Hope breathes deep into the heart of God's child, a voice of destiny calling out for them to succeed.

God empowers with His Spirit dwelling deeply within us. His authority is your authority; His anointing becomes your anointing. His faith in you becomes your supernatural faith in Him. When you grasp how wide, high, and deep His love is for you, you grasp a depth of hope that anchors you to God's holy throne. His hope will empower your heart to believe that nothing is impossible for God to do in you and for you. This way of thinking will move you from a slavery mentality into divine freedom. God has called you up; he has called you out! He is calling your name right now to go up higher. He wants you to come up higher with Him, having a much greater relationship than before. This is a deep, personal relationship with Father God, one that allows you to dance, be free, and live in the divine romance with God. He wants you to walk in a glorious freedom that overcomes life's obstacles.

Having the Lord's hope deep down inside of us will cause us to restructure our lives. It will remove our old "slave" thinking and replace it with "freedom and power" thinking. God desires for you to live in freedom with a consistent state of empowerment. He wants you to learn how to overcome regret.

When you walk in freedom, you learn to see your past from God's perspective. He sees your past as totally forgiven. It doesn't matter what you walked through, how bad your life was, or how many missed opportunities there were. God doesn't care about those. He cherishes the times when you stopped and acknowledged Him. He remembers the moments when you chose to love when being unlovable would have been a much better option. He recalls the moments when nobody was around and you chose to do what was right. If God had a memory bank that was just about you, He would bring up the files that remind Him of who you are—who He made you to be. He would bring up your image to honor and bless you. He would bring up pictures that remind Him of how wonderful you are. Like a good parent, He chooses to believe in you, regardless of your past. God chooses to let the bad memories fade, remembering the times where you showed Him that you depended on Him and His power, not what you could do on your own. God would recall the times in your life when you started to believe in yourself.

God Is Love, Not Condemnation and Fear

Why did God give mothers? To show the beauty, the tender loving care of who He really is—the most amazing Father ever. There will never be a God greater, higher, or more loving than our Father in heaven. Let this be applied to how you really see God. May you be overwhelmed by His personal love for you. If you were the only person on earth, God would have sent His Son to die for you. He loves you that much! His love is a reflection of who you are and what you really believe about yourself. You may have been told when you were younger that you were a mistake or that you weren't worth much. But when we rest in His tender, loving arms, we find His perfect love and peace. Like a devoted mother who would never abandon you as a child, God will never abandon you either. That is how I want you to see the Father, and that is how I want you to embrace His love for you. He chose you, loves you, and cares deeply for you. He wants every aspect of your life to be in HIM, permanently in Him and secured for life!

When you begin to look at God the way He looks at you, you will start to look at yourself the way He sees you. God sees you pure; now it's time to see yourself pure. What's in the past is forever forgotten; God will never bring something up that is covered under His blood. He covers it under the Lord's blood so that He can't ever see it again. If someone or something is bringing up your past, it's not from the Lord. God will never bring up your past to instill more fear or condemnation in you. That is NOT the Lord. It's Satan. God doesn't send tormenting messengers to you; it's not in His image to do this. God sends His healing truth and power. He sends you people who will help you understand how to live as a son or daughter.

You are NOT an Accident

Most of us were taught in school that we evolved from monkeys, but I have great news for you—you did not come from a monkey; you were created in the image of God. Animals have instinct—survival qualities without morals. Look at society and what's happening. After decades of this type of nonsense being taught as fact and echoed every day through TV, radio, and the Internet, no wonder so many people in the world feel hopeless and in a constant state of chaos.

Secondly, you're not an accident! It doesn't matter if your parents got together and did something they weren't supposed to and you were born by "accident" or by a "mistake" they made. It doesn't matter at all if you know or don't know your parents, if you were adopted, or completely abandoned on the street or in a shelter—YOU ARE NOT AN ACCIDENT! You are God-breathed and divinely appointed by the Father, Who loves you more than any other creation. He made you in His image—perfect in His eyes. I want to say this to you very clearly— God will *never* give up on you! Others may walk out and move far away, but God won't. He's always passionate for you and wants to be close to you.

Accidents may cause us to have inconvenience, but you are not an inconvenience to God!

We have to understand and actually believe that we are not an accident. So many people are walking through life, assuming that they are just some random form of an accident that wasn't supposed to ever happen. They get this from their parents saying things that should not be said. What's spoken out of our mouth will make an impact on the person who hears it. We have a lot of information floating around the Internet, news, and other places which doesn't line up with God's purpose and destiny for someone's life. For example, the public school systems teach kids through Common Core that we are here today through natural selection and evolution. When this type of false teaching gets into the minds of young people, it is like an evil cancer growing in a person's life; but in this case it is a hidden, slithering snake, designed to steal the future and destiny of that young person.

You are not an accident. You are not a mistake. You were born with a purpose and destiny!

You are not an accident. You are not a mistake. You were born with a purpose and destiny!

Every breath you have ever taken stems back to the breath of God breathing deep inside of you. This breath continues on to this day, and it will never fade. His breath won't fade, and neither will His love for you. The amazing thing about the Lord is that He never stops loving you. Not once has He ever thought of denying you His love. He doesn't cut you off because of your mistakes. He never walks away from you because of what you have done or who you have decided to become. All of the sin that you have ever committed will never separate you from the love the Father pours out toward you. (This isn't a license to keep sinning. That's not my point.) This is a license to love. God approves of you, period! He favors you! He isn't looking for a reason to punish you; He's looking for as many reasons as possible to bless you. His thoughts are always for you and His passion is always toward you. You don't ever have to second guess His love for you. You may not feel it, see it, or even sense His amazing love, but its right there for you. There's nothing more than God could ever want from you than for you to embrace His extravagant love. That is destiny dreaming for you. That is destiny speaking over you, saying that you will become all that God has for you.

CHAPTER 6: WHO AM I?

What Satan Wants

The mind can be Satan's playing field. The old expression, "I think I'm losing my mind!" is a common thought for many people today. That's because we allow so much into our thoughts, minds, and emotions through digital media. I think we allow too much to come into our thinking without filtering it first. Satan wants to infiltrate our thinking patterns in order to stop us from moving forward and stepping into the love affair with the Father.

Satan wants you to believe the lies; he wants you to walk in total defeat. If he can accomplish this, he wins because you end up forfeiting your divine destiny. Before we go any further, let's take a moment to deal with "the elephant in the room." These are things that nobody wants to address, but they are right there, sitting, breathing, and staring right at you. For this section, however, it's not the elephant that is causing the problem; it's the innocent, white lies that you have avoided or maybe you don't know how to deal with at all.

Time to Face What You've Been Avoiding

We've all got issues in life. You've got them and I've got them—things that you have to eventually deal with before it grows way out of control. Satan wants to distract your life so much that you end up becoming discouraged before you can even find out what you are really here to accomplish. Satan wants to keep you from discovering destiny's blueprint for your life.

What are your weaknesses—the deep sins and things that constantly trip you up, set you back, and cause you to feel shame? These are the tactics that cause you to feel unworthy, not good enough, or ashamed of who you are. These are the things that Satan will constantly use to make you see yourself as the exact opposite of who God made you to be. Satan wants you to feel defeated before you even begin. He wants you to believe you're defeated, dumb, incompetent, and not worthy of anything good, so that you won't experience the fullness of who Christ really is.

Believing the lies of Satan will cause you to start living them.

If Satan can lie to you, that's one thing. But if he can get you to believe the lie, then he has a foothold on you and it can start to control your outcome in life. It's like the old saying we've heard over and over again. "If you tell someone they're fat long enough, they might start believing it." Is that true or what? Satan wants you to think you are fat, odd, out of touch, not normal, so that he can get you to cower back in fear. Living in fear will destroy your faith. When your faith is destroyed, it will demoralize your future. That is exactly what Satan wants.

How many of your destiny dreams have been forfeited? How many times has Satan taken someone's passion, their identity to the grave? Believing the lies of Satan will cause you to start living them. If he can convince you that you're a chicken instead of an eagle, you'll never soar to the kingdom levels that God wants you to reach.

Stop Running!

Look at these questions and answer them. Be honest. You don't have to write it down, but I encourage you to take your time. Don't just read it and move on.

WHO AM I?

1. What is haunting you?

2. What is Satan using to torment you about your life?

3. What are some of the shortcomings, weaknesses, and struggles you are dealing with?

Now I want you to face them and let these words bring healing to you: Destiny dreams for you to become who you are in Christ. Destiny says that you're a child of God and nothing less. God will help you face some really tough things in life. His power will defend you; His honor will fight your battles for you. Through the heart of the Father, you will learn to listen to the voice of destiny and not the lies of the enemy. God says this about you: you're a child of the king—a lover of truth and wisdom. Most of all, He is the lover of your soul.

> See what great love the Father has lavished on us, that we should be called children of God! And that is what we are! The reason the world does not know us is that it did not know him. (1 John 3:1 NIV)

A love affair with the Father will begin to usher in the purest form of His identity for you. This one single act will change the course of your life more than anything else on earth. When I had my encounter with God back in the hotel that day, it cultivated my relationship with God in a way I never had experienced before. That is how He works, and that is what He wants to do for you.

Who is Christ?

When I look in the mirror, I see me—a mirrored image of myself staring right back at me. Without any distortions to the mirror itself, I will see my own image looking back at me.

When God created you, He created you in His image—a perfectly reflected human being without any flaws or distortions in the glass. When He created you, He made you in His exact image. If He is standing in front of a mirror, then you are the one reflecting back to him. Really—

you are a reflection of His heart and His perfect love. When light hits specifically-angled mirrors or objects, it will redirect so that the light is shifted another direction. When Christ's light touches you and works through you, it also redirects so that it will shift into areas of the world that could not be reached otherwise.

When you think about it this way, you see just how valuable you are in God's eyes. He doesn't make junk, and light never reflects darkness. God's light isn't meant to diminish your perspective about anything in life. His light is the brightest beacon within the darkest night. The hope that He shines will illuminate the deepest forest and calm the most dangerous seas.

> When God created you, He created you in His image—a perfectly reflected human being without any flaws or distortions in the glass.

What True Restoration Looks Like

Let's say you go to the junkyard and purchase a 1979 Chevy Nova. This car is completely beat up and sitting in the mud with no tires, no windows, the seats are all torn, and the hood is wavy. Most people would just walk on by that hunk-of-junk, rust bucket sitting two feet deep in mud that hasn't been moved for about a decade or so. Not to mention what kinds of little critters and creatures may be living inside of it of this metal bucket. Most would agree that buying a piece of junk like this would be a waste of time. You, however, have been looking for a 1979 Chevy and it doesn't matter what condition you find it in. You're a master craftsman and you can repair anything. But what you want the most, more than any car on earth, is the 1979 Chevy Nova. You can barely contain your excitement as you hand over the few dollars it costs to purchase it, then you pull it up out of the mud and have it towed back to your home.

96

WHO AM I?

Day after day, week after week, for months you continue working on this car that nobody saw anything good in. But you did. You knew all along that you could restore this car. You finished it off in less than a year. Spotless windows, a smooth, sparkling paint finish—but the real treasure of this car isn't the beauty of what's outside; it's what's sitting under the hood, an engine powerful enough to rattle the neighbor's windows. Originally the car came with a 350ci V8 170hp engine. You, however, dropped a 454ci big block under the hood. It starts quick and extremely fast moving past the finish line. With all of the modifications, you can probably race just about anybody with confidence. The interior is like a millionaire's living room with fully redone genuine soft leather seats. They are so comfortable, it feels like you're reclining in your living room. Plus, you installed perks that it never had coming out of the assembly line. You put in a better exhaust system, an updated computerized dashboard, air conditioning it never had, along with the newest custom design and racing technology to be found. You added a state-of-the-art heating system that gets it nice and toasty warm in just a few minutes.

Then comes the day when you roll out of the garage with your beautiful, recreated masterpiece. For fun, you take it down to visit the junkyard you bought it from. Eyes are popping and jaws are dropping once you're in the entryway of the gates. People are talking; they want to know where you got such an amazing car. When they find out that you got it from their junkyard, everyone is baffled. They are totally speechless at what you have done with this once-beat-up 1979 Chevy that used to be the collect-all for the elements, cigarette butts, and soda cans. Not now. It's the nicest looking car in the entire town. It sits low to the ground but slightly higher in the back. A little throttle on the gas turns heads and rattles windows. Everything works perfectly and is in mint condition. It's completely restored—better than when it came off the assembly line from the factory in 1979.

A Divine Restoration?

The state of this car is better than it ever was. This is restoration. Divine destiny is when God restores your life. He isn't thinking of what it

97

looks like right now. Instead, He is thinking of what your future holds and where you're going to end up once He is done working on you. He has a total makeover, a complete overhaul, in store for you. He has transformed your life so much that people who once knew you hardly even recognize you anymore—you're changed in every way. You're so different that heads will turn when you show up because the person you once were isn't who you are now. He has divine transformation for you. He has divine intervention, a blueprint from His throne directly to you, and only for you.

This is what He has for you. He has hope, a future, and a pre-determined destiny for your life. He hasn't made a single mistake in it.

> And if Christ is in you, the body is dead because of sin, but the Spirit is life because of righteousness. (Romans 8:10)

Destiny's blueprint will always lead you into the arms of the most wonderful Father.

It's Simple. It's Not Rocket Science at All

Sounds too easy to believe? Think about it. I'm telling you that you can have your best life now—not tomorrow or thirty years from now. Right now! With Christ, all things are possible. With God's heart toward you, what you may believe could never happen, CAN happen! I can tell you that because He has done it for me. I've watched God restore my life. He has made it better in every way. That is the Father's destiny for you.

Destiny isn't a far-off, distant event or occurrence; Destiny dreams can start a course correction at any time.

Destiny isn't a far-off, distant event or occurrence; Destiny dreams can start a course correction at any time. Destiny speaks, breathes, and gives life for you.

The word of God says that every step of the way God is there.

Yea, though I walk through the valley of the shadow of death, I will fear no evil; for You are with me; Your rod and Your staff, they comfort me. (Psalm 23:4)

God hears us and will respond.

Therefore I say to you, whatever things you ask when you pray, believe that you receive them, and you will have them (Mark 11:24).

We can go directly to the Father to talk to Him anytime and about anything!

What Have We Become?

When we think about where we are going in destiny, we should also include where we've been.

Regardless of how you feel about your past, God made no mistakes. He was there through all of the pain, suffering, difficulties, and whatever else you walked through. This is the tough part to address: God didn't do the horrible things to you. He's not that type of God. He didn't create you to torture you or to have you abandoned. He created you for intimacy with Him, a love relationship that grows deeper and deeper as the years go by. The hurtful, humiliating things done to you were not intended or intentional from God. They are a result of an evil world with evil people. But it doesn't have to end there.

Believe it or not, God can cause a lot of good to come out of a bad childhood. Some people have learned how to cope and deal with others or bad situations in life through learning how to deal with horrible situations while growing up. He can teach us certain coping mechanisms that will help us down the road. Don't get me wrong—coping mechanisms are usually for someone who is breaking down and doesn't know how to deal with life, so they start using drugs, alcohol, or resorting to bad things that only make matters worse. I believe that God works all things for the good, and God will use some of the things that

99

you had to go through for your benefit. God can take the bad situations in your life and use them to help you become a better person for your future. I haven't met one person in life who has ever said they had a perfect life growing up and also lives a perfect life now.

God can use the negative things in your past to build your future.

God can use the negative things in your past to build your future. He will take problems from your childhood and turn them around to bless your future. He is in the restoration business, and He can restore your life to be even better than it ever was before!

CHAPTER 7: ROYALTY

Have you ever met a current or former president of The United States? If not, imagine what it would be like if you were standing face-to-face with this type of world leader. Whether you liked them or not wouldn't be the point. The main focus would be the fact that you are standing in front of royalty. What would go through your mind? Would you be frightened or nervous? Common sense would tell you to not move quickly toward them unless they asked you to. Rest assured, once you got close to such a powerful person, there would probably be no less than five guns pointing at you from somewhere. That moment would feel both scary and breathtaking—something you would remember forever.

When it comes to royalty, both in the Bible times and today, and everyone has similar ideas about what royalty is. We think of respect, awe, amazement, honor, and also the realization that the person of royalty is in a very high position, one that we should respect regardless of our thoughts about the person.

I want to talk to you about a greater level of royalty: kingdom royalty. Our Father released His Son to earth to overcome evil and then return to heaven. In the meantime, Jesus releases His kingdom authority to God's children—you and me. With this power comes royalty. When we walk with God, we take on God's image, His royalty. Not His perfection, because we don't become as God, but we become a carrier of His anointing, which includes taking on the manifestation of His royalty.

He wants you to walk in His divine destiny and royalty. As a child of God, you are royalty! Your bloodline is the Lord's bloodline. Your past, present, and future have been redeemed. You may think that you're walking and living through a non-redeemable circumstance, but you aren't. You're walking in divine destiny with a loving God who wants to honor, respect, and treat you with the greatest love that you have ever known. More than anything else, He wants to be the lover of your soul.

> # As a child of God, you are royalty! Your bloodline is the Lord's bloodline.

You're a child of God, a son and daughter of the king. His passion is for you. His Destiny sees you as a success, not a failure. His love for you is endless, never fading, always consistent. You are His son or daughter. He will protect you with His life. He will overshadow you with His wings. He will guide you with His eternal light. In addition to this, He will instill in you His image and glory. This glory is living deep inside of you; It is eternally yours as a token of just how much God really loves you. God would never place His glory inside something that is not worthy. You, on the other hand, are worthy and honorable in the sight of God.

This is royalty!

The Image and Blood of Christ

The perfected image of who we really are can only be found through the blood of Christ. If we pull Christ out of creation, existence, and our destiny, we will only be living from day to day, just trying to survive. That is not how God wants us to walk. He wants us to carry out His perfect will for our life and help others fulfill what He has asked them to do, as well. This can't be done without Christ being the center of our lives. The center must include the perfect blood of Christ. Only the blood of Christ can change a person eternally. When we look in a mirror, we see a reflected image of ourselves. When God looks at us, He sees a reflected image of Himself. When we have Christ in our hearts, God looks at us and sees a reflected image of His Son, Jesus Christ. God doesn't look at our imperfections; He sees our completions. He is the writer; we are the pages. He is the sculptor, and we are the clay. God fills us with His lavished love. He becomes the lover of our souls—the passion for our destiny.

When His hands are placed on our lives, we discover our self-value. The passions He put inside of you are really from Him and no other. For example, God laid it on my heart to write a book—this book. He placed a call on my life to minister the gospel and to equip the church as He sees fit. This is something that is in my spiritual DNA, and God's Word says it is irrevocable. That means that it might shift from time to time, but it will always be my mission. Years ago, I was an associate pastor, now I am called to prophesy and teach others how to walk in their destiny. I'm the same person, still called to equip the body of Christ, but the focus has shifted over the years. Destiny is found between the "where you once were" and "where He wants to take you next" stages of things. What was played out through this process was accomplished by God's hand being placed on my life and His grace to accomplish the hard work that was set before me. How is this possible? God is omniscient. When He speaks over you, He speaks from His understanding and wisdom because He knows your beginning and your end. He is Alpha and Omega.

As long as you have breath, you have a destiny to behold! God is thinking of you; He is for you and never against you. Destiny speaks to you through the tender, loving voice of our Savior, Jesus Christ. Destiny clothes you through the gracious arms of our Father God, and destiny has forged you through the blueprint that is masterfully sketched by an all-knowing, all-powerful God. He wants the best for you.

Sons and Daughters

One of my favorite things to talk about is relationships. Having a pure relationship with God is what matters most. It's the greatest pleasure above everything else in life. When we humble ourselves, listen, and obey, we start to mature more because God begins to trust us more.

Destiny's passion for you—God's heart for you—starts beating faster and louder. Not because you have earned it, but because God sees that you understand it now. It's been there all along, but now you're grasping it. We mature more as sons and daughters that are now growing up. All the while, destiny is screaming louder and louder for you. Before long, destiny is crying out at the top of its voice for you. You are now living in the moment each day, walking in love-filled relationships with Jesus Christ. The cares of this world no longer bother you; the stuff that once upset you fades away because God's destiny over your life is speaking louder than any other voice around you. You are learning to overcome this life, and everything that is thrown your way is something placed back into the hands of our kind, loving Father. And with boldness and confidence, you can rest assured that God will take care of it; He has your back in every situation in life. Accepting the reality that YOU are a son or daughter of Christ and that YOU are made in His image is destiny screaming for you.

CHAPTER 8: DESTINY'S DNA

Relationships Matter

Good Connections

There are some good connections to have in life. Being connected to the right people can help you become who God has designed you to be. Destiny doesn't happen by accident. It doesn't happen through someone just walking alone, solo, through life. Destiny happens through divine connections. Every person who ever accomplished something life-changing has someone or some group behind the scenes rooting for them. Every great man had an amazing woman behind him. This goes for women as well; every amazing woman out there who has ever done something outstanding has people behind her who are rooting and cheering her on.

Things don't just happen by circumstance or happenstance, but through divine appointments and divine connections. When you see world changers, you don't just see people who did it on their own. You see people who had amazing individuals surrounding them. This is how I want you to see destiny. Destiny is dreaming for you through other people. It takes a team to accomplish something that is long lasting. Even if you did it or created something all on your own, you will eventually need a team to assist you with it. This team is destiny dreaming for your life. It's a divine connection for you to help you and the people around you to grow.

Bad Relationships

We've all been down this road before. We've connected with someone assuming that it was a great, God-led connection, to later discover that it wasn't. Relationships are vital; they are extremely important for how a destiny unfolds in a person's life. If we are not careful, we can connect with people who will bring us serious harm or trouble down the road. That is why it is so important to listen to the Holy Spirit in every step that we take in life, especially when it comes to who we should or shouldn't be connected with.

There are some people God will bring into your life, and the two of you will be completely inseparable and will remain loyal to each other until the end. You may have some trials from time to time, but the bond—the love for each other—is forged so mightily that nothing can separate you. These are the relationships that you cherish because they are often few and far between.

Then there are relationships that grow in different directions. At first there's a lot of trust, but somehow you grow more distant from each other. Maybe it's a move or a different direction that God sends one of you. In this case, you remain close friends, but not the best of friends for life. Your trust and respect for each other continues to grow, and tough times won't separate you or drag you apart; instead, your love continues with each step and phase in life. You're just not best friends.

Then there are bad relationships, which is what I want to discuss here. These connections may appear to be "divine destiny," but unfortunately, they are not. These are the ones which start off going well, but eventually it becomes obvious that the current relationship will not work. Something has changed, and it's not good, and it's not getting better. I believe all relationships can be restored; however, there are some that just need to be removed from your life. These are the bad relationships that you should not be involved with. In that case, it's better to move on the best that you can.

But I want to add one more type of relationship here: when you come into contact with a person who you just know in your heart you should not be connected with. It's not a good fit right now, and it may never work out. Sometimes there are things going on in a person's life that only God knows about, and out of His love and divine guidance for your life, He will tell you that you should not be connected with that person.

No matter what type of relationship comes into your life, it is vital to listen to the Holy Spirit with every one of them. Bad relationships can taint God's purpose for your life.

> ## Bad relationships can taint God's purpose for your life.

Your Destiny Isn't Defined by What People Think of You

With any relationship comes testing and trouble. It's not possible to have great relationships unless that relationship has become strained from time to time. Conflict will occur, and eventually some people might turn their back on you over things you never did. It might be a misunderstanding or that they simply no longer like you, care for you, or want to be around you.

I've had some relationships in life that I thought for sure were divine appointments—lifelong relationships sent from God. Sadly, some of them didn't work out, and, of course, people are still saying things about me that are not true. Why am I addressing this? Disappointment and betrayal come with the territory of developing great relationships. Through the process, some may try to define you as something you're not. Some may even attempt to lie about you or manipulate you to be a person you're not cut out to be. These are toxic relationships because they will eventually destroy your destiny. You are *not* defined by what people think about you, but rather by how God sees you. Remember, you are made in the image of Christ, God's Son.

He is the image of the invisible God, the firstborn over all creation. (Colossians 1:15)

Your Destiny Isn't Established by What Others Want You to Become

You've heard the story before. A young child wants to be an artist and their parents just don't see it. The father wants the child to become a lawyer and the mother wants the child to become whatever the father wants them to become. In this specific home, the father directs—or should I say "dictates"—everything that goes on. Deep inside, the mother wants what's best for her son, but the father believes that power and money rule the earth, so if his son is going to be successful, he has to be a lawyer like himself. Besides, the father has done extremely well in his practice over the last twenty years, so he can train his son in all legal matters. In his mind, it will be a great business partnership with his son; someday he will retire and will need someone to carry on the family practice. But there's a hiccup in the mix—*God.* God placed it in the son's heart to become an artist, and he could become an amazing one. The parents don't see it yet because it hasn't been revealed. God, in His perfect ways, has plenty of time to work out the details and kinks in this scenario. Eventually the son grows into a mature man of God and goes off to school to become a digital artist. Sometime later he is working with an animation company and is making more money than his father ever thought possible with an art degree. The son becomes established as a renowned artist, and his family accepts it and him as part of a divine plan handed down by God.

We can go on and on about stories like the one above. Maybe this happened to you, where someone has tried to make you become something that you're not. Maybe you chose to follow a career path that isn't really where you should have been.

Destiny isn't defined by where you've been or what you're currently doing. Destiny is defined by the hand of God establishing your life. The

Father loves you enough to erase the bad choices that you made in life to restore your calling. He wants to take the misstepped places and turn them around to be His steps toward His destiny for your life. You are not defined by what others want you to become. You are defined by what God has called you to be. That is destiny dreaming for you!

> Destiny isn't defined by where you've been or what you're currently doing. Destiny is defined by the hand of God establishing your life.

Your Will or His?

Do you know what is most likely one of the biggest roadblocks on the path to your destiny? It's YOU! Yes, I said it. You're the problem; you're the one to blame! Maybe I stepped on your toes just now, but I did it for a reason. This may be true for some of you reading this right now. Sometimes the thing that stands in your way isn't what people think of you or what someone is trying to get you to believe or do. It might be what you have chosen to believe about yourself. I'm not referring to lies that Satan has thrown at you; I'm referring to your will against God's will.

Have you ever had someone talk with you about a specific situation they were facing, and after they told you about it, you felt as though God was giving you specific directions to tell them? You listened carefully to everything they said, but while listening, you knew in your heart that you had an answer from God for this person. You weren't attempting to "play God," trying to solve the problem for them, or trying to steer them in a direction that would benefit you in some way. You were hearing the voice of God and you knew it. At the end of the conversation, you were led by the Lord to give them your advice, and to your excitement they said, "That's exactly what my other friend said, and my pastor, and my mother. But that's something I just can't do."

What? Not only did you get the same thing from God for that person—it was the same exact thing that three other key people in their life had already spoken to them. None of you talked about it; in fact, you don't know those other people at all. Sadly, the person didn't listen and they ended up going their own way, fully knowing that there would be dire consequences because of their decision. They are now following their own will instead of God's. They have intentionally placed God's will behind their own. That is what I'm referring to.

Sometimes the biggest problem is ourselves. We hear what God is saying and choose to ignore it. Our own will, our own mindset, has clouded destiny's dream for our lives. Our will can really create some serious failures for our lives and others, which can hurt our destiny. It's nothing God can't later fix, but there will probably be some delays for the next few years to fix the mess we created by not listening to God. If you're in this situation right now, look up and know that God will forgive you for not listening and He is more than willing to fix the mess you're in. His love for you is unwavering!

So Where Do We Start?

Let's start with a few questions here:

1. What has God said about your destiny?

2. What do you think about it?

You see, God is the direct link to your destiny. He is the divine destiny, the power that rests behind every step you take in life. You are the conduit; He is presence (the energy) behind what drives you. What you have, He has put within you. He is like the stream of living water flowing through you, and you are like a pipe or a water channel that moves and directs His streams as He desires. When it comes to your destiny, God is dreaming for you. Without Jesus as the center of His will for your life, it will not happen. Destiny's dream for you is completely centered on Jesus. Jesus's passion for you is centered on His desire to be with you. There isn't a substitute for time with Jesus. Nothing else can satisfy the way Jesus can.

Jesus IS the Center

We start with Jesus as the center. Is Jesus the center for the passion you carry? This is most important. If He isn't the center for what you desire, then what is at the center that you desire most? Is it your own plans, a successful career, or an important relationship? Maybe it's a hobby, or other things like that. For some people, it might even be the desire to have a huge ministry. To fix this, we have to turn our attention to the love of the Father. We must place our efforts, desires, and passions into the hands of Jesus. Sometimes the hardest part in doing this is learning to trust Jesus and knowing that God will finish with what He started within you—and that it will be good! Find out what is really in the center of your life. Christ wants to be in the center and with no other.

> In exchange for you giving up your life to honor Him, God will bless you by giving you the desires of your heart.

When we place our trust in the Lord completely, we lose control of our will and allow His will to take control of our life. You might be passionate about one specific thing, but He may redirect or channel your passion a different way, making it more for His glory and less for yours. In exchange for you giving up your life to honor Him, God will bless you by giving you the desires of your heart. He knows what's best for you and what you really want. He knows how you can live for Him, while at the same time learning to live for who you are in Christ. It's funny how we have to let go of our life in order to gain it back. Who gives it all back? Jesus.

For whoever desires to save his life will lose it, but whoever loses his life for My sake will find it. (Matthew 16:25)

111

CHAPTER 9: THE DNA OF YOUR PASSIONS

What is DNA?

There is a code—a unique, individual code—for every person on the face of the earth. This coding is what makes us who we are. It defines our hair and eye color, our racial identification, our gender, and thousands of other identifying factors that makes us different than anyone else. What is it?

Deoxyribonucleic acid, better known as DNA. Guess what? The same way our physical bodies are coded to be a certain way, our passions also have their own sets of unique coding. To better understand how this works with our passions, let's take a closer look at physical DNA.

The Importance of DNA

Deoxyribonucleic acid is a material present in almost all living organisms. It is self-replicating and is what chromosomes are mainly made up of. DNA carries genetic information and determines the fundamental and distinct qualities and characteristics for each person. Without DNA, there wouldn't be anything unique from one person to another.

The main role that DNA plays is to provide a genetic instruction guide by storing information within cells. It is a vital aspect for everything living, even plants have DNA to dictate what type of plant it will be. DNA contains instructions for every cell in each organism's development, reproduction, and even for its death.

Just as you have DNA that only you carry and no other person on earth will ever have, so does God. It is through His Son, Jesus. When God created the world, He made no mistakes—no plan B. He knew we would sin and He knew that part of His divine plan would involve having His image come to earth to redeem the entire world. This would only come through His son, His DNA, to the world. In the same manner, He chose to use you—your DNA and His DNA working through you—to touch the world. You are also a part of His plan for this world. You are just as important as any other person who has ever walked on this earth. It doesn't matter how old you are, where you live, or what kind of mess you're in. It doesn't matter to God because you are a part of His DNA. You're living because He created you and breathed His life into you. That is how amazingly personal God really is. That is how deeply He loves you.

> ## You are just as important as any other person who has ever walked on this earth.

With His DNA in your life, His passions for you become your passions for yourself, as well. What He placed in you before you were born is what God wants you to one day become. The hungers that are deep inside really count. Your desires really matter to God. He placed that DNA code within you before you were born.

The Power of Passion

Let's talk about passion. Passion is the power that allows you to accomplish what others can't. The perfect example is Michelangelo's statue of David.

In 1501, at twenty-six years of age, Michelangelo was commissioned to create the statue of David. Typically, David was pictured in triumph after his battle against the famed giant, Goliath. However, Michelangelo decided to go a different direction; he chose to picture David *before* he battled Goliath. The passion he carried for this project was like no other. Though it can't be proved, it has been said that Michelangelo worked on the huge seventeen-foot-tall, over twelve-thousand-pound slab of white marble for two years before revealing the final creation. Furthermore, the block of white marble that was used to carve David had been worked on more than fifty years earlier by Donatello, but was said to have had a flaw in it, so the project was abandoned. That for sure shows the passion within Michelangelo for King David's statue!

What others couldn't finish, you will. Why? God's DNA lives inside of you, and this DNA carries passion.

Passion Breaks Barriers

The word *passion* refers to emotions that are strong and barely controlled. To have passion means that one has very strong feelings or beliefs about something or someone. We all have passion about something, and it's very important to tap into our passion for God.

When heaven's DNA of your passion ignites within you, it will start to break supernatural barriers. There is a passion deep within you, and that "hunger" is directly linked to your destiny. God puts within you what you are called to be. Deep within you, He places the code for who you really are. God is faithful to establish who you are and what you are called to be. What He placed within you before you were born is what He wants. This deep call to persevere past anything else is destiny dreaming for you. When we step into God's dreams, we have the ability to break the "sound barriers" of the voices around us that no longer belong. Time to break the barriers!

Breaking the Sound Barrier

Chuck Yeager, an American test pilot, became the first person who was able to break the sound barrier, which is the point where a fast-moving object (like an airplane) surpasses the speed of sound.

115

On October 14, 1947, Yeager made his famous, record-setting flight in an airplane that he called Glamorous Glennis, named after his first wife. The model of the plane was a Bell X-1 rocket plane, and it exceeded Mach 1 after dropping from a B-29 airplane.

The supernatural sound barrier for your life can be broken by the power of Christ working through you. Chuck Yeager didn't know what to expect when he broke the sound barrier because it had never been done before. This is also how it will work in your life. You don't know exactly how things are going to work out. You've prayed about it, you've planned, you've even contacted people to get advice—but you are still walking by faith with God on a road you've never been down before. It is an exciting journey!

This is the power of passion in your life. It's what drives you to get up in the morning and stay up late working on what you love to do the most. It's what causes you to love someone when in your mind you want to hate them. Passion can turn a person's life totally around. God is passionate about you and He wants you to continually thirst for Him as you walk in divine purpose for your life. This is God's calling speaking, living, and fighting for you.

> Passion is what drives you to get up in the morning and stay up late working on what you love to do the most.

The Difference between Desperation and Passion

There seems to be a thin line between desperation and passion, which we need to be able to distinguish if we want to live passion-filled lives for the Lord.

Desperation

Have you ever panicked before? Desperation is like being driven into panic mode. The person has nowhere else to go; they have nowhere to turn. They are willing to do anything to get free from the situation that they are currently in. That's what makes desperation so dangerous. People who are desperate can bring harm to themselves or others.

But there are times when God allows us to become desperate for Him. It's like having a thirst for God for life, which is still within the scope of passion, and there's nothing wrong with being desperate for God. However, God doesn't call us to walk in "panic mode," always chasing fantasies and heading one step further into another disaster. That's not true passion. Passion isn't fear-driven or a last resort in life.

Passion

Godly passion is really the pursuit of Jesus. It's a love affair with the Father as we walk through life.

God responds to passion because He loves to pursue His children. He also responds to desperation because He cares. Have you ever been deeply moved to help someone simply because they are desperate and crying out for anyone to help them? Then you come along, and in your heart you know that the right thing to do is to offer assistance. That is how God works; He knows that deep inside, you really need help, so somehow He'll make a way for you. That is how destiny starts to dream for you. When we know God is trying to woo us, it causes destiny to start dreaming again.

I want to point out something here. God is *not* desperate. God is *never* in a place where He is desperate, because He is flawless. To be desperate, you must be in serious trouble and need a lot of help. God has never and will never be in serious trouble; He doesn't need help. Instead, He chooses to receive help by working through people like you. On the other hand, God is desperate for *you*, and more than anything, He wants to be close to you and to have a personal connection with you that is stronger than anything else on earth. That is how desperate God is for you. That is how deeply God loves you!

117

False Desperation Leads to Religion

I don't want to mislead you here. A world-driven or false desperation on your part can lead to bad choices. This happens when someone is desperate for something like drugs and they are willing to commit any crime to get their next high or fix. This type of desperation is dangerous and deadly. Desperation from God toward you is what I'm referring to in this chapter. God is desperate for you because He loves you. He chooses to be that way for you. He doesn't want you to live in a constant state of desperation for Him. This results in a strained relationship. When someone focuses so much on desperation toward God instead of falling in love with God, it can become a form of religion, or an act of worship out of duty (false desperation) instead of a lifestyle of love toward God.

Let me illustrate this another way.

Let's say you visited a church that started over sixty years ago. When you walk through the front door, you quickly notice that the building looks more like an antique store with "old time" relics all over the place, memories, and plaques from the past that aren't relevant to the current state of their city or town? After you go into the church the service begins. All songs and hymns that are being played were popular several years ago, but none of the songs are relevant for today, for this generation. You look around and notice that nobody in the congregation is from the younger generation. It's just the older generation present and all of the young people are gone. You begin to think, "When did religion move in?"

How did this happen?

It can happen to any church, denomination, fellowship, or person. In fact, it can happen to you and me if we allow it. We can get so comfortable with a system that worked in the past that we no longer allow God to give us new patterns or systems that are relevant for reaching the newer, current generation. Each generation has a certain style, culture, and way of doing things. Likewise, Jesus is always relevant to culture, and how He speaks to the next generation may not be exactly how He spoke to your generation. So instead of adjusting to where God is taking you

118

now, you settle in on where God *took* you several years ago—and you camp out there. You pitch a tent that was supposed to be temporary, and instead you make it permanent. God didn't call you to tent living; He called you to increasing glory and kingdom dwelling. A tent can't contain all that God has for you, and too often we live in the "temporary" too long by trying to force it to become permanent. That is how the glory moves out and religion moves in.

Religion convinces you that you're being humble, when you are actually bound with religious chains.

When we allow religion to move in, our identity and destiny become tarnished. We start living by performance and less by relationship. Your identity is now based on your performance. It may look good, smell good, and feel good, but deep inside, there is something terribly missing. Performance-based relationships will always leave you empty. Only God can fix this; only He can turn your false identity (performance living) into real identity (destiny living).

Religion convinces you that you're being humble, when you are actually bound with religious chains.

The good news is that we serve a great and mighty God who knows how to deal with Jezebel. You see, during this stage in my life, God knew all along that I was going to go down into a deep dark pit that was being led by this Jezebel spirit, but God saved me and my family. He delivered me, casting her away once and for all. Jezebel doesn't have any right to function in my bloodline anymore, and now I can detect her from a mile away. I know how she controls because she once controlled me. This is the goodness, the gracious mercy of an all-loving Father. He is willing to look past our weaknesses, our strongholds in life.

When we understand His love for us, His light will radiate through us. It can take some time for God's love to set in. For example, I used to be a "fire and brimstone" preacher when I first was saved, but it was because I didn't know who I was in Christ and I didn't fully understand the Father's love. Once the power of intimacy with Him touched my life, my message changed from "get right" to "get married to Jesus." Religion and legalism left and intimacy moved in forever. My life now is all about intimacy and getting to know Him. Intimacy isn't something like a job or a work project, something that we just do to get it done. Intimacy is relational—and it gets better and better as time goes by. Our identity is no longer about what we do, like ministry or business; instead, it's all about who we are in Christ.

Destiny Dreaming Is Moving from Performance to Presence with God

We lay down our lives for Him. We want Him much more than any gift He can ever give us. We live for His relationships more than anything else in this life. I think it's going to be so crucial for what's coming prophetically in the world we live in. People who take time to know Christ personally will live different lives compared to people in the world. This is destiny, to fall in love with Him. Destiny dreams for you; you are the Father's delight made perfect within His hands.

Destiny is found in a love-relationship with Christ. Destiny is lined with humility. When we humble ourselves and seek His face, He will keep us in a right-standing relationship with Him. God will say "go this way" or "go that way," and we will humble ourselves, trust Him, and obey. This is always the right pattern for our lives. Humility will never leave you empty or abandoned.

> For the Lord takes pleasure in His people; He will beautify the humble with salvation. (Psalm 149:4)

CHAPTER 10: THERE'S A PRICE TAG ON YOUR FUTURE

From Darkness to God

On August 20, 1994, I had a drug overdose, and that's when I met the Lord for the first time. Factually, I was paralyzed; I had no feeling in my arms or my legs. During this encounter, all of the sin that I ever committed was flashed before my eyes. I lay there motionless. I was with my brother, and I didn't even know who he was. I didn't know my parents either; it was as if my parents didn't exist in my mind. My mind couldn't function properly. The only thing that existed was this dark evil—my sin—right in front of me. Every possible thing that I'd ever done wrong, willingly in public or even in secret, was flashed before me. It was like having an encounter with a Holy God who knew every single thing and detail of my life, and now it was all being unveiled for the entire world to see. For me, I just saw all of my sin. There wasn't anything discreet about it. It was real; it was horrifying.

That moment was when I asked Jesus to come into my life. I decided right then and there to give everything I had to Him. What happened next will actually floor you, and some reading this may think that it sounds like heresy. But I am telling you the truth of what happened, because it is the *real truth* in someone's life that will set them free. So here's the truth.

The very next day I actually smoked marijuana while I read the Bible. For a long time, that's all I did. I would have flashbacks. Through this crazy experience, the result would always lead me to know and understand just how good God was and how good God is because He spared me. As the marijuana and Bible-reading moments continued, I saw and discovered more and more about the goodness of God, and I kept being reminded that God freed me. He saved my life! This thought about how God saved me just kept reoccurring to me over and over again during this time. Eventually the Lord helped me to realize that drugs and the Bible don't mix. He led me to a Benny Hinn event, and it was there where the presence of God fell upon me. After returning home I went back to my old ways and smoked pot again. The Lord spoke to me and said, "Sal, I really don't want you smoking pot anymore." So I asked him, "Does that mean I have to be a preacher?" This was how walking with God began for me. I began to get serious about my call.

For example, my circles of friends changed. I was never drunk again. I never got stoned ever again. For some of you reading this, it doesn't line up because it doesn't fit into your "box." For me, this is exactly what happened, and this is how an all-loving and gracious Father reached out to me, was patient with me, and caused me to want to know Him passionately. If you've never been addicted to a substance before, you won't understand the powerful satanic force that lies behind addictions like drugs. But God understands—and He met me when I needed Him. That is destiny dreams.

God Is Serious

Having the drug overdose was my warning. Around that time was when I really got serious and wanted to know the Lord. For me it was more than just knowing Him. I was asking, "Who are You?" and "You created me; now I want to know more about what You are about."
What drove me deeper and deeper to Him was the fact that He spared me. I would often ask, "Why did you spare me? Who am I that you

THERE'S A PRICE TAG ON YOUR FUTURE

would save me from destruction and, ultimately, death?" These are some questions that I chose to dig deep within myself, and I recommend that you take time to ask God the same types of questions.

When I looked back and saw what He did for me, it drove me to want to know Him more. His passion toward me drove me deeper to Him. That is how God works. That is destiny speaking loud and clear.

Following God Will Require Effort

Look at what the Bible says about love:

> And though I bestow all my goods to feed the poor, and though I give my body to be burned, but have not love, it profits me nothing. Love suffers long and is kind; love does not envy; love does not parade itself, is not puffed up; does not behave rudely, does not seek its own, is not provoked, thinks no evil. (1 Corinthians 13:3–5)

Love is a choice, a decision that requires effort. Your destiny and growing a relationship with God require cultivation. That is what I came to realize when I stopped smoking marijuana.

> Your destiny and growing a relationship with God require cultivation.

When I asked God if I had to become a preacher, He really didn't answer. It came to me as an inner answer. From that point on, He put something in my heart, because I always knew that serving Him more was what He really wanted for me. I knew I was done with marijuana. I knew that becoming a preacher wasn't a big issue because I wanted to give my life over to God anyway. I wanted to serve Him for the rest of my life. I always wanted to speak for the Lord, and within a few years, I was praying for people, something that came naturally to me by then.

I didn't have the lighting or visitation that told me to start preaching; I just knew in my heart that this was what God wanted me to do.

As I started off walking with the Lord, I had to learn how to keep pride out of my life. I began walking in humility and the love of the Father. For starters, I started to see my dad and my family the way God saw them. I had to grow up and stop depending on my dad as much. I had to "die to myself." I was used to doing what I wanted, and getting what I wanted, whenever I wanted it. But God had other plans. He taught me how to honor my father and mother much greater than I ever could in times past. This is how God works in a person's life. He will cause you to start seeing the destiny of other people, and not just yours. God will develop a love within you that's on fire for others around you.

Here are some questions to consider:

1. When was the last time you prayed for someone else other than yourself?

2. How long has it been since you went out of your way to help someone in need?

I believe the one area that marks God's church (His people) more than any other is the fact that we are called to love. We are called to serve others. To be direct with you, we are called to love the unlovable and forgive the unforgiveable. That's what marks us as true sons and daughters. Love and forgiveness are the gems within us that set us aside from all other people on earth.

When we start to see God's perspective on these issues, we also begin to realize just how much we used to get in God's way. This is one area I struggled with: being in God's way! I've learned to slow down in life and let God lead me the way He wants. I've discovered how to take His hand through all circumstances, to trust Him in every detail. When we get in the way, we mess things up. It all boils down to control. Who is in control: you or God? If we can learn to ask this question in all circumstances, we will come out on top more times than not. God wants the victory in every area of our lives. He wants to see us overcome this life, not be defeated by the problems the world gives us.

When we get to this place (honest trust) with God, it's nothing shy of a miracle. Learning to lose control so that God can take control might be one of the toughest battles in our lives. Let's face it: there are some things in life that we don't want to lose control of. Even after we are saved for a long time, we still may want to keep a tight grip on certain things. The enemy says that you have to keep control of something or you will lose it. But the Spirit says, "Learn to let go and trust Me." This is destiny for you! Destiny is letting go of our control in order to reach the fullness of Christ. We can't have a partially controlled life blended with a totally controlled life with God. It won't work. God wants us to rest in His unconditional love. It's the most purified walk with God you can ever envision. When we release our fears and failures and take God's love in exchange, it's like destiny crying out for you. His passion for you combined with your passion for Him becomes an unrelenting force. That is something that darkness can't ever remove from you. That is His heart. That is when destiny starts to come alive again.

> We can't have a partially controlled life blended with a totally controlled life with God.

Look Who's There—Jesus!

Now it's you and Him, and you look back on your life and realize that God gave you a chance. In fact, He gives us all several chances in life. The greatness of the God we serve is based on the fact that He is a God of mercy and grace. He's the God of multiple chances. Religion gives little room for mess-ups and mistakes. Religious people will throw you out, but God doesn't—He will pursue you over and over and over again. This is God's work of "sonship" within your life. It's being a son and being a daughter, regardless of everything else going on. We see that in parenting. It doesn't matter what your child does; that child is still yours. They always have and always will be. That is how God sees you!

As a son or daughter, your true identity will emerge. Your real DNA—who you truly are—will come forward from within you. You will walk through life as a gift sent from God, as one being "sent" and not just someone on the go all the time. Your life will become more productive and less busy, because busy people produce very little in life. Here God teaches us how to slow down, walk in His steps, relax, and trust Him to the fullest.

Jesus also teaches us how to follow His steps. When we follow Jesus, He will keep us relevant in everything we do. Jesus is always about relevance and culture; He is never outdated. He is in the center of life and the issues that matter most to people. He sees us the way the Father does, which is perfected, full of His glory from the beginning. We are predestined for greatness, for destiny. We're not predestined for destruction. Death and destruction are reserved for the wicked, not the righteousness of God!

Relationships Matter

Destiny is all about relationship. It's about choosing to put down what matters least and pick up what matters most. To God, you matter most! This is His heartbeat and passion for you. At no time was God ever against you. Not once! When we see the genuine truth of the love of the Father, we can't help falling in love with Him. When God opens up His heart and exposes His glory to us, the result is that we fall in love with Him. It's a real, truthful love affair with God—something we will talk about in a later chapter.

CHAPTER 11: DESTINY DREAMS FOR YOU

N ow, let's get to the greater good: Destiny dreams and how it affects you. Destiny has always been dreaming for you. Before you were born, destiny was alive and well in your life. Destiny is God's breath being exhaled inside of you; it's God's hope being implanted within you. But it doesn't stop there. He continues to give you golden nugget after golden nugget throughout your life. God was always dreaming for you to get into the loving arms of a gracious and protective Father. When I look back, God was always giving me little nuggets here and there. He would always figure out creative ways to drive me closer to Him. It took a long time for me to finally understand this and how it relates to destiny. For God, destiny isn't here today and gone tomorrow; instead, destiny was before you were born, is currently happening now, and will be long after you're gone. Your destiny in Christ lives on forever! Not only will you live with Christ forever, but what you sowed, watered, and reaped on earth will remain until the Lord returns and at that time what you built for the Lord will remain for God's glory.

Destiny dreams for you because it was predestined for you. You were already called to walk in your destiny way before you even got there. The DNA assigned to your life was coded specifically so you could become who you are in Christ. Look at the scripture below.

For those God foreknew he also predestined to be conformed to the image of his Son, that he might be the firstborn among many brothers and sisters. (Romans 8:29 NIV)

The Father Will NEVER Abandon You

Sometimes people may tell us that they feel as though God abandoned them because of what they had to go through in life. Let's be honest, but also sensitive to some reading this. There are some really evil people out there. Years ago, for the most part it seemed like tragedy happened far away. We would read about or see news about someone who killed someone else in a faraway state. That's not the case today as we discover that evil is lurking in every city and town, large or small. There are some really bad people out there today doing some really bad stuff to people.

Bad people are hurt people. A bad person didn't wake up one day and decide to become evil. They were hurt, wounded, and abandoned by those they deeply trusted. Bad people are nothing more than deeply wounded or hurt individuals. Sadly, some people have been entangled with these evil people, and for some, what we read about or hear on the news is what they are actually walking through in real life. Evil has increased, just like the Bible says it will. There are some really great people out there who have had some really horrible things happen to them—things no person on earth should ever have to go through or face in life. So the question becomes: Did God abandon them?

The answer is found right here:

> Let your conduct be without covetousness; be content with such things as you have. For He Himself has said, "I will never leave you nor forsake you" (Hebrews 13:5).

Satan wants you to believe that you were abandoned by God. Satan uses this tactic to turn your heart from God, the loving Father. God doesn't turn His back on you, but Satan will. What the Devil likes to do is turn against you by working through evil people on earth. If he can

128

bring harm to you through the workings of bad people, then he can try to convince you that God doesn't care for you or love you. That is what the devil wants.

You see, God will never turn on you or stop loving you. His love is unconditional.

You see, God will never turn on you or stop loving you. His love is unconditional toward you. But Satan can convince you that you can't trust God anymore because He doesn't love you. We have to continually remind ourselves that this isn't what the Bible says in Hebrews 13:5. The author of Hebrews is actually quoting from the Old Testament in Deuteronomy 31:6, where God spoke to Joshua as the Israelites were getting ready to cross over the Jordan River into the Promised Land. The promise here is the fact that God will never leave you, which is a kingdom wealth that surpasses any other fortune on earth. The focus here isn't on if we should have money or not; the focus God is pointing out in Hebrews is that we have an incorruptible kingdom of wealth that can never be taken from us. When we place our hope and trust in His kingdom glory instead of our earthly treasures, we get a guarantee from the Father that says, "My son or daughter, I will never leave you nor forsake you. So put your trust and hope in me." This is true destiny, it's a kingdom destiny that will never be lost, stolen, broken, or removed from your life. This leads me to the Father.

Destiny Dreams Is the Father's Love for You

Destiny dreams is what will lead us into the loving arms of the Father. This is the heart of the message for this book. The Father's heart for you with destiny dreams is learning how to walk in your true identity. You can only do this when you understand the Father. There isn't another way. As your relationship with Him goes deeper and deeper, the revelation of who God is becomes clearer and clearer.

Remember when I mentioned that God always hides things for His children to later discover them? I also mentioned that God placed golden nuggets into my life all along the way, even when I wasn't serving Him. He was still speaking to me, trying to woo my heart to His. This is the loving passion that the Father has for you and me. This is the importance of discovering the true identity of who you are and Who He is. There's only one key—and that is intimacy. Having intimacy with the Father is the single most important thing you can do. When this becomes a day-to-day reality with you toward the Father, you realize "Wow! You're my Daddy!" You will start to realize that God the Father wants to have a personal relationship with you. It's the idea that *he wants you!* He is all about you. He loves you and desires you more than any other created being on earth. That is how crazy God is over you.

Your Daddy Is Crazy for You!

Do you recall when you were young when someone that you really loved came home? For example, some of you may remember your dad coming home after working all day and one of the first things he did was to pick you up and hold you. Or perhaps it was another relative, like your mother or grandmother. The moment they walked in the door, it was all about them and you—nothing else mattered. Your toy racecars or dolls were strewn all over the floor, but that didn't matter now—grandma was here! And oh, the love she had for you because she hadn't seen you in over a week, and a week was way too long for grandma! She gave you the feeling that if she didn't get a hug from you soon, she would burst and be no more. Do you remember having relationships like this with anyone? Most reading this do, and if you don't ever recall having a relationship like this, then I pray with all my heart that you will soon. God wants to fill the void within your heart.

This love relationship you had with your relative was pure; there wasn't an agenda. Just the idea of spending time with each other was what mattered most. All you wanted to do was be around each other. This is how God sees you. His thoughts toward you are always delightful, never tarnished or impure. His love toward you is like an unbreakable seal around your heart.

His thoughts may look like this: "I love you! I can't wait to see you again, to place My arms around you and love you forever. I am dreaming for you; destiny is awakened within you because of My love for you. I would never want anything bad to come against you or ever hurt you. This is My love for you. This is My unwavering promise to you. I am your protective Father, you are My son or daughter for eternity."

God can't wait to start leading you into destiny. This is His love-passion for you. He is delighted to watch you grow and become who you are in Christ. That's what destiny dreaming for you really is. It's the Father's heart that creates the destiny. And that's how destiny dreams because of Daddy's pure desire for you. He is your Papa!

A Royalty Mindset

> Oh, the depth of the riches both of the wisdom and knowledge of God! How unsearchable are His judgments and His ways past finding out! (Romans 11:33)

God's ways are not man's ways—God's ways are always much higher. No one person will ever fully understand the mind of God, because He is God and we are small humans compared to Him. We are the created, so our thinking cannot ever reach the full capacity of how the Creator thinks. That would make us "like God," which we aren't. Regardless of how much we try, we can only slightly understand who God really is. God's sovereignty allows us to discover who He really is. You see, destiny is so powerful that even your ability to screw the whole thing up for yourself is limited. God's knowledge and perfection is so far above who we are that even if we attempted to mess things up, we will still be limited in doing so. He allows us to search out the "unsearchable" because of His love for us. This is royalty! We don't deserve it, but He gives it anyway. We shouldn't have it this good, but God makes it better for us anyway. This is royalty!

131

The scripture above is referring to the fact that we really can't understand everything about God; in fact, we are too "unholy" to even go near such a holy God. But because of His goodness, He lets us into His chambers for a love relationship with Him. His ways are past finding out, but from time to time, He reveals them to us because of His great love for us. That is when we humbly draw near to Him.

God Dreams for you

Have you ever met a visionary? After just talking with them for a short time, you realize that this is someone who has big plans, and they are probably going to accomplish them by the end of their life.

It has been said that the late, great Steve Jobs changed the world one computer at a time. His vision was to get a personal computer into every home. This would allow every person to have the opportunity to learn and grow in knowledge. Well, he has pretty much almost accomplished that; and if not in every home, then for sure on every modern phone. What a vision! That is what it's like seeing real vision come to pass. Though Steve Jobs has passed, his vision for making technology easily available has transformed the entire world. It has also changed how we "do church" and are able to share the gospel to the masses around the world with just a click.

People have vision and they have passions. If you stop and talk with any person on the street, you will discover that they have a passion deep inside. Something is tucked within the heart of every person on earth. That something—that vision—is from God. It's a desire to accomplish what God has set in motion for that person to work hard at. That is how God sees vision. That is how I want you to see yourself.

God is always dreaming for you; He's passionate for you. His desire for you is to have the ability to be able to reach way beyond what you think you can accomplish. He wants you to be able to speak in front of people you never thought you would be able to reach. God wants you to envision things that can only be accomplished through miracles. That is God's heart for you! He wants you to see yourself as more than willing and able. He wants to watch you set world records, invent things never yet thought of, and write truths that have been recently revealed. He wants you to build homes and vehicles that have completely new engineering. God wants you to discover things on earth that have never been discovered before.

Something is tucked within the heart of every person on earth. That something—that vision—is from God.

Not everybody is called to the same places in life. This is the beauty of the body of Christ. It's God's ability to use you and other people to reach others that are unreachable. He wants to use you through your creativity. What? That's right! God wants to use you through the creative nature that He has placed within you. He wants you to think out of the box in such a way that your thoughts become revelation that will one day lead to a revolution. God is a visionary; He sees you from the beginning to the end. He is also a revolutionist.

That's it; God's a radical. He wants radical and eternal transformation in your life and everyone around you. Think about it: look at how many times Jesus stepped into a scenario and just "messed it up." But did He really mess it up? No! Jesus stepped in and made things fall apart because they weren't meant to be that way to begin with. Jesus stepped in and turned things upside down for some people, but in reality, He turned them right side up because He was making things how they were supposed to be, from a kingdom point of view. Jesus is a radical. He is radically in love with you and He wants every part of you. He dreams for your destiny day in and day out. He wants nothing less to be able to say to you, "Well done, good and faithful servant!" He wants to say, "I love you, My son or daughter; you have finished the race set before you." This is destiny dreaming for you. This is destiny awakening deep within.

Destiny Cries for You

We talked about the difference between desperation and passion already, but I'd like to reinforce this concept one more time. Why? You can't walk in your calling if you're not passionate for God. You have to be "desperate" in a healthy way toward the things of God, meaning that you're not at your wits' end—instead, you are pursuing God as an only option or plan. There isn't a plan B.

Desperation versus Passion

To me, a desperate person has nowhere to turn. They're in panic mode. If you're passionate about something, you're ecstatic and you have purpose. When you're desperate, your purpose in life can go right out the door because you have nowhere else to go. Before I was saved, that was how I felt. I had no purpose. I was hanging around my friends, doing drugs, and partying, but I wasn't having fun. What I was doing was numbing the pain, avoiding the void; that is what drug users are really doing. Eventually, I got to a place where I was tired of doing things my own way. I was tired of operating out of my flesh, tired of having to solve my own problems in life. I didn't want to do things my way anymore. Back then, everything I did was a mistake because it wasn't properly placed in the hands of God. I became desperate for God to set me free. I became desperate for a move of God in my own life that would change the direction for myself and others forever. I think sometimes God uses our desperation to refill our lives with passion. I was really desperate. And when you're as desperate as I was, you are willing to try anything to get set free. I believe God saw this and He responded to my desperation, my heart's plea, my heart's cry.

Deep inside, I didn't realize just how passionate God was toward me. When I started to realize this, it increased my passion for Him. Then I became passionate. Why? Because I know what I'm called to be—I'm a son. I have stepped into sonship. I'm an heir to His kingdom. So I'm passionate to see God's hand work through my life. I want to see God's hand working in everybody around me, too.

134

Now I carry a new sense of desperation. I am not falling apart and willing to try anything to get free. I'm already free! I'm desperate now because I live such a passionate life for God that it's like an animal running in the wilderness with little water. If they don't get refilled over and over again, the animal will dehydrate and die. That is how I see God's passion toward mankind. He turns our serious problems (desperation and despair) into radical love and passion; this is what causes us to become passionate about Him. It becomes a long-term love affair with Jesus.

God's Call and Passion in Your Life Will Break Through

So now what? God is redefining who you are on the inside. He is causing people around you to notice that you are becoming confident in the decisions that you're making now because you are confident in who you are in Christ. This is initiating a deeper confidence in where you're heading in life. But you are realizing that how you got to this moment won't be exactly how you will get to your future. If you keep doing what you did to get right here, right now, you're only going to end up in the same place (where you are now) twenty years from now.

Right now, destiny has become manifest. It's making itself known in your life. Vision is becoming a reality, not something that is really far away. You're starting to see and believe that God can work supernaturally through your life, so things are starting to change. Some people may be starting to feel impatient, as if God isn't moving fast enough. Nope! God is right on time. He is working things in your future and on your behalf that you have never thought of before. And now it's time. God has laid on your heart that major change is coming. It's time to do things like switch careers, move to another city or state, take on a new job, or go back to school to further your education. Whatever it is, it's big. It's a big step in life! Yes! Its time. It's something that's got to happen—and change is in the air now.

This is the moment of breakthrough. You have a choice. Some people will cower back and retreat because the thought of starting over or going through something like this is not pleasant. This is also where champions of destiny are discovered. This is the moment of decision, and it is at a divine time and place in your life. Will you keep doing what you're doing, or will you make a God-led, divine decision that will change the course of your life forever? That is the real heart of the matter. Are you willing to trust God with breakthrough? Are you willing to take the next step—one of the biggest steps in your life—to show God that you are willing to trust Him with everything?

I'm not talking about stupid decisions that are just "fluffy" desires that you want to do. I'm talking about divine steps that the Father Himself, has laid on your heart, and you know it's time to take the next step. When you do, it's time for breakthrough! Breakthrough comes when you step out in faith. When you are led by God to climb a mountain that you know you can't scale without His help, it is breakthrough.

Destiny dreams for your breakthrough. Destiny longs to see you break something open that will change the course of your life and for everyone who ever comes after you. This is destiny! God doesn't want to watch every generation that comes up after you to have to deal with the stuff, the sin in the camp that you had to deal with and destroy. He wants to watch the generations that come after you walk in a level of breakthrough that nobody has yet been able to walk in your bloodline. God is in the breakthrough business, and He is passionate about seeing you break through the walls that contain and refine you. This is destiny busting open doors in your life that were once sealed shut.

God is that good! He wants to have a spiritual love affair—a relationship so good that it surpasses any other relationship known to man. It's this relationship that will bust open the doors of destiny in our lives. You can't get this type of intimacy through a weekend retreat or conference. This type of relationship only comes through time with the Father.

CHAPTER 12: TIME TO DREAM

L et's talk about dreaming. We all have dreams in the night from time to time. Since the encounters that I have had with God, I have lots of dreams at night where God speaks to me. This has been steady, and seems to increase every so often. God gives me a lot of revelation in my dreams, very important information about others, my surroundings, and people I might come into contact with one day. God can use your dreams too. It's His will for you to be refreshed when you sleep and that your spirit is awakened by the presence of God actively speaking to you within your dreams. Dreams can change the course of a person's life, they can serve as a warning, or to inform you about something you wouldn't have known otherwise. Dreams are God's way of speaking to our spirit man while our brains are functioning at a lower capacity than when we are awake.

Albert Einstein's Dream of Relativity

Albert Einstein once received a dream that changed the entire course of science as we now know it.

In 1905, a 26-year old Albert Einstein spent his days working for a patent office in Bern. On his off-hours Einstein toiled away at developing his scientific theories, eventually producing articles that were published in the prestigious journal, The Annals of Physics. In these articles Einstein postulated a radical new conception of space and time, arguing that the relationship between the two is relative. In other words, Einstein outlined what would later become his theory of General Relativity.

To be sure, Einstein's ideas grew increasingly more sophisticated as he developed them in time, yet one can trace the whole of his scientific oeuvre to an experience he had long before he became a full-fledged theoretical physicist—long before he even wrote his 1905 articles. In fact, the kernel that led to Einstein's concept of special relativity came to him in his childhood dreams.

What was the dream that so inspired the young scientist? It actually had nothing to do with the stars or the cosmos—it had nothing to do with the sky at all. Rather, Einstein's dream was a pastoral fantasy set in the Alps, complete with a cast of farmer and cows. The story goes that Einstein dreamt he was high in the mountains one misty spring morning, walking alongside a stream that trickled from the snow covered summits. He walked until the mountains parted and valleys came into view. Einstein could see fields, some of which were cultivated and divided by fences, and realized that he was moving towards civilization. Nearing one of the fields, Einstein noticed a small herd of cows huddling near an electric fence. Some of the cows were munching on grass, their heads slipped through slats of the fence, unhindered by electric current. Curious, Einstein neared them. As he approached a farmer came into view. The farmer, Einstein quickly realized, was tampering with a battery. Within a matter of seconds, the sadistic farmer had activated the electric fence, causing the cows to retreat in terror. From Einstein's perspective, all of the cows jumped into the air at once, scampering to safer ground. The farmer, however, violently refuted Einstein's claims, insisting that he had seen the cows jump in the air one by one before fleeing the scene. The rest of Einstein's nightmarish dream consisted of a prolonged back and forth between himself and the farmer; an irresolvable dispute regarding the reality of what had just occurred.

Einstein awoke, perplexed. Why had he dreamt of cows? More importantly, why had he engaged in such a dispute with the farmer—could it be possible that they truly had, based on their unique vantage points, experienced time and space in different ways? Einstein has said that the rest of his lifelong career may be considered an extended mediation upon the questions inspired by the dream of electrocuted cows. It makes one wonder how many dreams that we've written off as absurd and meaningless might have warranted a bit of extra consideration...[3]

It couldn't have been written better than what Lara Andersson wrote about Albert, and how this one single dream affected his life so much that he studied the science between space, time, relativity, gravity, and movement for the rest of his life. Was God speaking to Albert here? I would say so! God knew that Albert would use the brilliance He had given him to discover certain sciences in the early 1900s that had never been thought of before. God also knew that some of the things Albert would discover later would change the course of how science and research is conducted. Albert's dream created something in him that birthed destiny in his own life. It also caused destiny to be birthed in many others.

Though we can't tie what Albert studied and proved scientifically directly to the single abovementioned dream, we can see that his studies changed the world of science forever, from understanding the size of a molecule, to providing research that backs the atomic theory, all the way to the famous $E=MC^2$, which is used to prove how much energy is released or taken up during different nuclear reactions.

What if everyone had a life-changing dream like Albert's? What would have happened if Mr. Einstein had just gone back to sleep that morning and completely ignored the dream? The one dream that changed the course of his life and many others and impacted science for centuries is the dream that Albert acted on. Albert could have just let it all go and

3. Andersson, Lara. 2014. *Invented in Bed: Einstein's Theory of General Relativity.* July 1. Accessed 2019. https://blog.casper.com/einsteins-theory/.

moved on to something else. How many dreams do we get like this in life that we take for granted, treat with contempt, and just let go?

God's Dream for You!

What I want to talk to you about right now isn't necessarily a dream in the night. I want to address a truth that I believe will direct the course of your life toward divine destiny. If you can grasp this one thing out of this book, this one concept in this chapter, then I believe you'll become effective in fulfilling the call of God on your life. This life-changing truth is that if we could ever get inside the mind of God and take a look at what was really going on inside the divine King's mind, I believe that we would see images of you and me moving through His thoughts. I believe that He would spend most of His time thinking about *you!*

There has never been more passion discovered than the passionate love God has for His creation—that is, you and me. And if we were to look inside the mind of God for just a moment, seeing all of the images, we would see images of our lives flash before us, but we would also see our image in the future. God wouldn't be focused on all of the mistakes that we've made over the years; there wouldn't be any pictures up there on the walls of His mind about the failures, the sins, or the big embarrassments that we had to go through. Nor would there be any videos of us walking through tough times without anyone to help. What we would see is God dreaming for us. We would see images of what God believes we will be several years from now, who we will be with, and what our life will be like then. He would have before His mind thoughts about our successes and what He has had the honor of leading us in life. We would see ourselves as "fulfilled" on earth—and that is how God would choose to see us.

He wouldn't look at us as the slender, skinny little runt who once threw tomatoes at cars on a dare. Or the time we cut off our brother's hair or our sister's Barbie doll hair just to see how it would look. Though some of those things might be funny to look back at, He would choose to see us in your completed form, the image of His child through His blood working in you. God would see us as "covered," not abandoned or alone. This is God's dream for us. This is destiny dreams!

Destiny Dreams Is When the End Becomes a Better Beginning

When we grasp the idea that God's thoughts are always toward us and that they are good thoughts, not for harm, it will change the outlook of our lives. Our lives will shift. The end of the line for how we once lived becomes the beginning of a new legacy for our future. An era of defeat fades while the birthing of a new dawn begins.

> When we grasp the idea that God's thoughts are always toward us and that they are good thoughts, not for harm, it will change the outlook of our lives.

For instance, what if at the age of forty or so, God decided to redeem the last twenty years of your life? He takes all of your failures and bad decisions and overwrites them, causing them to all turn in your favor. Or it's like getting a letter in the mail from your bank or the IRS, saying that there has been a mistake on their part and they owe you over $10,000. This is the type of favor God will place on you. These are the types of things that will happen when we allow His dream to become ours. There comes a renewed sense of hope that overflows in our lives. It's so lively that it's captivating for anyone who comes near you. Something is different inside of you—and that is the dream of God being placed deep within you.

Destiny Will Stop What Doesn't Belong in Your Future

When we allow God to take over, destiny takes the lead. Something supernatural occurs, because what was meant to harm you will now bless you. It's like having a toy train in the house. Setting everything up can take several hours to several days. One part of the track gets popped into place while another part comes loose. During the first few test runs, the locomotive doesn't go completely around because there are flaws in the track; maybe the wiring is loose somewhere, or maybe the track isn't completely level. Eventually everything is put into place and the train makes its way around the track over and over again.

In life, there are things that can delay the events in our lives from unfolding properly. It's here, however, when we give everything over to God, He takes the broken pieces of our lives—the disconnected tracks—and connects them properly to get our lives moving again. In some cases, God will allow the old train to wreck so He can give us a new train to start over with. A train wreck occurs because the bad train isn't allowed to follow you any longer. The bad train was cargo from your past and train cars from the previous generation. This train was fully loaded on a mission to destroy your future. It followed you wherever you went, and with every bad decision that you made, the speed and power of this train gained momentum. This train was on assignment to destroy your life and bloodline. Then destiny dreamed about you, and through sovereign intervention, it busted the track.

> God will not break His word with you. He will fulfill everything that He has placed within you to accomplish His promises.

Destiny will derail the bad train that tries to follow you. This train can no longer go into your future. There is a line there, and the bad train isn't allowed to cross over it. From that moment on, the good train, the whole, completed train for your life, starts to go with you and before you. It's the Lord's train; He is blazing a trail for you that no other person could ever fulfill in your life but Him. God has great plans for your life. He has a future filled with promises that have already gone before you.

142

God will not break His word with you. He will fulfill everything that He has placed within you to accomplish His purposes.

Heaven SHOUTS for You

> Therefore we also, since we are surrounded by so great a cloud of witnesses, let us lay aside every weight, and the sin which so easily ensnares us, and let us run with endurance the race that is set before us. (Hebrews 12:1)

It gets better, though. Life doesn't stop with just fulfilling our destiny on earth. That's just the beginning of it all. Life continues with an eternal covenant with the Father, all of us living in eternity forever. That means that we get to see all of the amazing purposes in life completely fulfilled. You get to look back at your life on this earth and see how it really unfolded through the perspective of God's divine eyes. Just the thought of that gets me excited! One day, we will hear the glorious praises of His people and the sounds of angel's wings within the skies, along with the four living creatures crying out before the throne. What a sound to be heard and what a sight we will see! While we are still here on earth, we will get a small glimpse of the glorious riches of God, like flashes of His greatness being revealed as our destiny unfolds.

Heaven is shouting for you. Look up and see the glorious clouds of heaven as millions of people form the great cloud of witnesses all cheering for you. All of those who went before you will recognize that you're there. They are worshiping the King while waiting for you. One day you will see them and the Lord face to face. This is the beauty of God's passion for you. The things that you will go through on earth are nothing compared to the greatness of eternity in heaven. This shows just how good God really is. This shows His eternal love for you that once you are finished on earth, He is just starting with you. He sees you through the eyes of eternity, a completed masterpiece now formed for His glory and honor—a human being who He will eventually spend eternity with. Nothing can overshadow this hope He has built within us. This is destiny crying out for you! It is an eternal longing to be with you.

Intimacy and Compassion

When it comes to the Father's passion and dreams for you, it's not possible to understand this without intimacy. If you know anything about me, you will know that I'm all about intimacy with the Father. I am so much about intimacy, that my wife, Kristine, will sometimes tell me that I actually have a "feminine" side to me. What she means is that I have a love for the Father and for others. I'm gentle, truthful, and firm when needed, but my heart is filled with compassion for others. This is all part of a romantic walk with God and learning to walk in intimacy with the Father.

God never called us to be calloused on the inside. He called us to be compassionate. Compassion gives us the ability to show concern or sympathy toward the hurting.

What Is Compassion?

Webster defines *compassion* as, "Suffering with another; a sensation of sorrow excited by the distress or misfortunes of another."[4]

In simple terms, you're the person who stops to help someone when everyone else walks by on the other side of the street. I believe one of the greatest powers on earth—love being the greatest, of course—is the ability to have compassion for people.

The church is only as strong as its compassion for those outside of its walls.

> So Jesus had compassion and touched their eyes. And immediately their eyes received sight, and they followed Him. (Matthew 20:34)

---

4. *Webster's Collegiate Dictionary*, s.v., "compassion," (G. & C Merriam Co.: Springfield, 1913). Public Domain.

We see over and over again in the Bible how Jesus was moved with compassion, so He fed, healed, or delivered the people around Him. God is moved with compassion toward you. Jesus is compassionate. He feels the sorrow, the pain, and the suffering of those who are helpless, and He fights for them. If you want to get God's attention, watch how He responds to the hurting and helpless. He is the defender of those who can't help themselves. Our King is moved with deep compassion toward His people. When we take on this same compassion toward mankind—God's creation—supernatural breakthroughs will occur. If you get a chance, do your own study in the Bible about how Jesus was moved with compassion toward those who were sick, hurting, and hungry. The power that rests behind miracles isn't as much the "supernatural" as it is compassion toward the hurting. The flame that keeps miracles moving is created by the fuel of compassion.

> # The church is only as strong as its compassion for those outside of its walls.

To have a love affair with Jesus means that we must put Him first and be with Him as one of the highest priorities in our lives. To have this relationship, it requires intimacy (vulnerability)—being able to be "laid out bare" before Him. This isn't in a clothed or non-clothed sense; it's more about our feelings and thoughts being made known to God. When we come into the presence of the King, we must be laid bare, nothing standing between God and us. We must be honest and truthful with how we are really feeling, not attempting to hide anything (laid bare). This will only happen when we are moved with passion for Him. When we are in the presence of the Lord and passionate about God, for who He is, and not what we can get from Him, there will be an end result: compassion for people. We can't have a calloused heart and work for the Lover of our Souls. We can't have a hard heart and serve the Maker of the Universe. Compassion and intimacy go hand in hand. You can't have one without the other. This is destiny for your life.

Before moving on to the next chapter, answer these questions:

1. Are you moved with compassion like Jesus was toward the hurting and helpless?

2. What moves you the most?

CHAPTER 13: LIVING OR KILLING THE DREAM

Have you ever thought about how many people in life really live the dream? In other words, they can truly tell you that they are living the best life a person can ever live. They have done some things that maybe no one else has ever done before. Maybe they have walked through some doors that became opportunities that changed their life. These types of people are intriguing because there are few people on earth who will say they are honestly living the dream.

If you talk to people while you are out and about, the majority of them will say that they wished they had a better life. Then they will often talk about moments in their own past where they had one missed opportunity after the next, which is their way of justifying how they got where they are today. They allow excuses to justify why their life didn't end up the way that they were hoping. For some, I get it; things happened outside of their control, and it shipwrecked a large portion of their lives. I also get the fact that nothing is impossible with God, and I know that He can restore the worst of situations in a person's life. I know this because He has completely restored my life, and if God can do this for me, then He can do this for anyone.

As I mentioned earlier, God is *for* the helpless, the outcast. He wants to take a person who has shattered dreams and dismantled hope and turn their life around for His glory. In fact, I would go as far to say that God LOVES doing this! Why is this? Because He is genuinely in love with His creation—you and me. So is it possible to "live the dream"? Absolutely! It's possible to be in the center of God's will and remain in love with Him at the same time. This is living the dream in God's eyes. But before we get there, I want to share a few ways that will destroy—or kill—your dream. I want to remind us all that it is possible to destroy your dream simply by doing some of the things mentioned below.

Killing the Dream

Refusing to Extend Forgiveness

Forgiveness isn't the same as trust. It's possible to forgive someone—for example, a rapist—but still never get into a parked car with them ever again. Another way of putting this is you just don't trust them at all and you never will. When we forgive someone, we pardon them. That doesn't mean that you let the robbers back into your house. Nor does it mean that your abusive boyfriend can come back into your life. If you forgive them, you extend grace to them; you pardon them and you're not carrying hatred or bitterness with you anymore. You have let it go. But you may never trust them again.

> # You will kill your dream if you refuse to forgive those who have wronged you.

People need to understand this because if not, relationships will get confused and stressed out because they are filled with unnecessary tension. If someone wrongs you, God will help you forgive them, but it doesn't mean that you have to trust them. We've all had to learn to forgive people, but we also have to set up trust boundaries as well. Forgiveness isn't *trusting* them; it's *forgiving* them. Forgiveness and trust are not the same. You can have one without the other. You will kill your dream if you refuse to forgive those who have wronged you.

> Let all bitterness, wrath, anger, clamor, and evil speaking be put away from you, with all malice. And be kind to one another, tenderhearted, forgiving one another, even as God in Christ forgave you. (Ephesians 4:31–32)

Repentance

This is keeping with repentance toward God. Another way of putting it is sanctification. This is the process of becoming holy *after* we become born again. Being really direct, it means that God knows that you and I will still screw things up long after we are born again and saved by the Lord's blood. He knew it before and after your salvation. You and I will do something that we know in our hearts is wrong; it will still happen. Whatever it is, we are eventually going to do it because we live in a fallen world and we are not immune to temptation just because we are Christians. Somewhere, somehow, we are going to mess something up, and we will feel really bad afterward.

At that moment, we have to stop what we are doing and ask our gracious Father to forgive us of our sins. Not the sin of being unsaved—God already dealt with that and He doesn't have to deal with that one again. You are a child of God for life. God knows that you will still sin in some way after you are born again, and He expects us to talk to Him about it when the time comes. This is what it means to keep with repentance. It doesn't mean that we keep asking God to save our soul again; it means we are asking God to forgive us of the stupid thing (sin) we just committed, and we decide that we are going to turn from that sin. We have to keep with repentance to prevent killing our dream.

De-Tangle Your Lifestyle

Remember the moment you got gum stuck in your hair? It's happened to all of us! Remember how grabbing one part of the gum and pulling only made matters worse? With a few more tugs, most of your hair was tangled right into the massive gum wad that now had to be cut out. Yup, you were six years old and you had what appeared to be a bald spot on the side of your head. Embarrassed, you laughed and then cried. But the next day, the bald spot was still there. Eventually, your bald spot grew out and blended in with the rest of your hair, and things got back to normal— play time without anyone poking fun at you.

In our society, media has portrayed that a lifestyle we once thought was immoral is socially acceptable now.

Maybe your life was doing well until you met the woman across the aisle in church a few Sundays ago. At first she seemed ladylike, innocent, and Christian to the core. A few dates here and there, a few passionate kisses, and then before you know it she's sleeping on your couch— knowing darn well that this is NOT good. You know that it will probably lead to you calling in late or "sick" tomorrow. Not to mention the "elephant in the room"—sex is *probably* on the horizon. You ignore the matters at hand; you ignore the Holy Spirit urging you to tell her to go home, and before you know it, things have been done that you can't reverse.

Fast forward a few more months. You discover that she's now pregnant and she has confessed that she can't tell exactly who the father is—you or the four others she slept with around that time. But she swears that she loves *you* and nobody else. Could it be that you have the highest paying job of the other guys? Before long you are in a mess that could have been avoided.

What happened? Just six months ago you were one year from life-changing destiny, now your life has completely fallen apart. The answer is your choices. In living for the moment, you bit the bait of Satan, his kiss of death for your destiny and God's dream for you. The results are now catastrophic for your life and others around you. This is how Satan works—and this is what he wants. He wants to entangle your life like the chewing gum that was in your hair as a kid. He wants to create such a mess that your life has to be "cut out" or even cut short. There is only one solution to avoiding a situation like this and that is to *detangle yourself!* Do it *now!* If you know it's not good, it's time to let it go. If we don't detangle our lives to avoid situations like this, we can destroy our destiny. That is what Satan wants.

Living the Dream

We've just seen a scenario on how to kill your dream. Now let's take a look at how to live your dream. To recap a few things we have discussed already, I would like to point out some simple ways to live your dream. There will be more about this topic in a soon coming chapter. For now, let's take a look:

Become Who You Are in Christ

First and foremost, we must become who we are in Christ. This is the first option, and there isn't another option after it. We have to search out who we are in Christ by discovering who Christ is. At this stage, we have to be upfront with God. What is it about our life that we do and don't like, and where are we really heading? Next, we have to be upfront with ourselves. For some, this will be a huge reality check. This is where we discover *what* God has really called us to do. At first, it might not be what we want to hear. We must be upfront and honest though. Destiny dreams with honesty.

> # We have to search out who we are in Christ by discovering who Christ is.

Once we get this down, we have to look into what others are trying to make us out to be. We have to be upfront with others, letting them know that we are not going down the same path we once took with them. This might involve making appointments with people so that you can be honest with them. God will probably show you some people you can't walk with anymore, and it can be hard to tell them. For some of you, it might be a close friend, a company that you've worked for years, or a family member God doesn't want you associating with anymore.

I'm not advocating that you just cut someone off or walk into your day job tomorrow and tell your boss you're leaving. This isn't the key to destiny. I'm encouraging you to be upfront and honest with God, yourself, and others. It's the other part that you're going to have to plan out and think through, because you don't want unnecessary repercussions from spouting your mouth off too early. Timing and precision are really important here. You don't want to get fired because you told your boss too far in advance (like nine months) that you wanted to leave one day. Know who you're supposed to talk to and the timing of the conversation.

Don't Take It Personally

When you start to walk in truth, you will soon rattle those around you who have been living a lie with you. This is hard to understand, but sometimes those around you love the fact that you are more "bound" than they are. Sometimes, people around you are the ones who have been holding you back all this time. So when you become truthful and freed up deep within and start walking in your destiny, you will rattle some religious cages around you. Some people will turn against you because they don't want you to walk in the fullness of Christ, destiny's cry for you! I know this sounds crazy, but it will happen—and you have to be ready for it.

Even Christians who are close to you may become naysayers— people who don't want you to succeed, or perhaps don't see the vision of where God is leading you. This is okay; you may still be their friend, but God might tell you to move on. Some, on the other hand, love you and may become concerned that they won't have time with you anymore or they may not see you much in the future. In this circumstance, the person might be emotionally attached to you and they will just really miss you as you move on. You're going to have to ask for wisdom in all of these circumstances. You'll have to walk in a lot of grace and tender mercy. If you don't, you can become bitter. As you say your goodbyes, keep before you the idea that this is only a season, and you're heading toward your destiny now. Take no offense to anything during this time.

Redeem the Time

> Redeeming the time, because the days are evil.
> (Ephesians 5:16)

Last but not least, the main way to live your dream is to redeem your time. This has to become a central focus in our lives in order to walk in the destiny God set before us. When we look back at all the time we wasted over the years doing things that hurt our destiny, there emerges a sense of urgency within us. It's something deep within that tells us we have to make the most of every opportunity. When we are passionate about something, that is what we should focus on.

One way to redeem our time is to be willing to say no to everything that doesn't matter anymore. When we are focused on our true destiny, we don't have the time to waste on other things. We have to learn how to say no to the things that matter least and yes to the things that matter most. The way we redeem our time is through keeping our eyes focused on what God has called us to do. Placing accountability on our lives, schedule, and time are really important; if we don't monitor it, someone else will take advantage of it for us.

Getting the clutter out of your life will allow you to flow and function out of intimacy with God.

God wants to see your time redeemed. He wants to restore all the time the enemy took from you. He desires to give back to you some of the best years of your life. When you see His goodness, how incredibly loving God really is, that is what will drive you to want to work for Him with all of your heart. It's what makes you willing to say no to everything else on a regular basis. Getting the clutter out of your life will allow you to flow and function out of intimacy with God. God's will for your life is to further His kingdom, and this will require commitment and precious time.

We are sons and daughters, His precious treasure. He takes delight in watching us restore broken dreams and lives around us. He takes great pleasure in watching us pursue His purposes. God is for us, never against us, and always pursuing us.

CHAPTER 14: A LOVE AFFAIR WITH JESUS

I was in a coffee shop talking with a friend of mine who is a minister about some of the topics in this book while it was being written and my friend asked me, "So what is your book really about? Can you sum up your book in just one thought?"

I instantly said, "It's all about having a love affair with Jesus." My friend's eyebrows rose upward as his curiosity peaked. I could tell he probably hadn't heard of that one before. Honestly, I'm not sure I'd ever blurted it out that quickly either.

As we were sitting there in the coffee shop with other people all around us, I continued, "Jesus is my lover—He's the lover of my soul. He handles all of my affairs in life the way He wants. I want Him to have total and complete control of my life in every way. This is far more important than any church, ministry, or family role or obligation." I could tell that he could see that God was working in me. Jesus was doing something new in my life and in the lives of those around me. When we draw close to God, programs will fade and presence with Jesus will last forever.

A love affair with Jesus is so real! It isn't something that we watch in a Hollywood movie; it's something you can live in reality right now. Over and over, God says in His Word that He is for you, not against you, and that He wants His best for your life. He also tells us that He wants to be with us more than anything else on earth. This is destiny dreaming for you! This is the heart of God bringing you into the fullness of His love. He loves you more than anything else! It's possible to be fully in love with God.

Heavenly Encounter

I want to share a story with you about something that happened to me a long time ago that caused me to realize just how much God loves me.

Years ago, I had an angelic encounter with God which would later help me to understand just how important healing and deliverance really is. It's what led me on the path to destiny. I was a student at a supernatural ministry school, and I went to a conference put on by the school. While I was there in a hotel room, I was asking God, "Why can't You just use me in ministry? How long do I have to wait? I want to launch; I don't want to do anything else for the rest of my life."

Notice my cry? This is before I knew my real identity. I started praying and meditating over a passage in Revelation where it talks about Jesus' hair being as white as snow (Rev. 1:14). As I was meditating on Jesus, I was suddenly taken by the Holy Spirit and translated into a glorious and heavenly place that eventually looked (to me) like a nightclub without any people in it. This nightclub wasn't secular; it was just filled with glamour and splendor. While I was there, I saw an angel starting to walk toward me. I was awestruck. As the angel came near to me, it tried to touch my shoes. It caught me off guard, so I started to back up because I would not let it touch my shoes. Behind me was a stairway going up, so I started backing up the steps. The angel reached out to touch my shoes again and I maneuvered to avoid having him touch my shoes a second time. Then in a flash I was right back in my hotel room.

The Shoes

I asked, "Lord, why wouldn't I let the angel touch my shoes?" Then God began to unfold to me the purpose of this encounter. He showed me that my shoes represented taking the gospel to the nations. They also represented being prepared for the high calling God had for my life.

God has to have His way in you in every area of your life, or you won't be able to fulfill your divine purpose. The divine romance with God is like a dance where God is leading you and you are following Him. Our feet must be anointed, willing to go wherever God leads them.

I would like to point out something before we go any further. It's important to note that God wouldn't release me into a greater capacity of ministry before showing me the encounter. This was because before this encounter, I wasn't walking in the fullness of Christ.

> # The divine romance with God is like a dance where God is leading you and you are following Him.

The Stairway

When I stepped backward up the stairway, it was God's way of showing me that someone has to be willing to mature, not at the pace we want, but at the standard and timing God has set before us. Every step you take up the stairway of heaven is one step closer to becoming more mature, more like Christ. Each Christian is different and on different steps, or levels. That is what makes the body of Christ so beautiful; we are all constantly growing upward toward the glory of the Lord, and every new step is a new sign of maturity in your life.

More to the Story?

Did you notice something odd? During the encounter, I was going up the stairs backwards because I was trying to keep the angel from touching my shoes. This is extremely important because it was intended to reveal something to me that I hadn't seen before. The divine romance with God requires us to leave what is not important behind—and that is what the dream was all about. We come to Christ and we start to mature in the Lord, but there are some things that we're not willing to let go of. I was going up the stairs backward, attempting to back away from the angel trying to touch my shoes. This was very symbolic because what God showed me is that this was how I was living out my life at the time, and this is how many people try to live with the Lord.

Sometimes we try to go up the stairway of heaven backwards because we don't want to give God control over every area of our life. The angel was trying to touch my shoes, but couldn't because I wasn't ready for that yet. I was avoiding it at all costs. I had neglected to deal with some things in my life, and that is why the angel couldn't touch my shoes. It was also why I was going up backwards instead of forwards—I wasn't looking toward the glory of the Lord by going up backwards. God's divine love affair wants every part of us—He wants it all! He wants to propel you into a romantic relationship with Him that is unlike any other.

> Sometimes we try to go up the stairway of heaven backwards because we don't want to give God control over every area of our life.

Help is Always Needed

I started to seek help after that encounter. I began to ask the Lord to deliver me from any type of spiritual or demonic influence that might be in my life. I really wanted to know why I didn't let the angel touch my shoes. This prayer and cry to God went on for months, and during this time I had many other spiritual encounters, which all happened to show me how important it was to be truly honest before the Lord. For me, this meant that I needed special help from a deliverance ministry. It took me a while to find the right person who actually understood where I was coming from as a Christian seeking deliverance and not someone still out in the world not walking with God. Years later, I still talk with this person about situations that come up from time to time. For me, having a Christian counselor who is seasoned in the spirit realm in deliverance and healing has been one of the best things in my life. It's what has helped me to become more like Him, learning how to live in a truly romantic, non-threatening relationship with God.

Broken and Restored

All of this led me to a place where I was willing to tell God, "Break me, remold me. Use me." I needed to become bankrupt of everything—every pattern and cycle that was out of the will of God for my life. I realized that I needed to be totally washed clean with no more hidden areas in my life.

During this time, I was having more and more angelic encounters. I even had bizarre encounters with actual people who were being "translated" into my house. If you are not familiar with the spiritual occurrence of translation, it is when the Spirit of God moves someone to a specific place for a specific purpose. This happened in the Bible (see Acts chapter 8), so it shouldn't surprise us when it happens today, but it is something that blows our human minds. God can transcend time and space, which is hard for us to comprehend, but He can do it.

These people would come into my room in the Spirit and when I would see them again, they would tell me details about my room that they couldn't know because they had never been over to my house (except when God brought them there!). They would describe in detail where the doors were on the walls in my bedroom and colors on the walls in my home. These individuals had never been in my room before; some had never been in—or even near—my city. It was astonishing! But more importantly than describing my room, these Christians would give me timely words from God that confirmed to me that God knew what I was walking through.

This brought me into a deep revelation of the love of the Father. The fact that God would send people into my home in the Spirit to get a message across to me spoke to me deeply; in fact, it took me into a closer walk with God, because I started to realize right then and there just how personal and loving our Father God really is.

Destiny Is a Love-Relationship with the Father

Presence

So what does this boil down to? PRESENCE! God doesn't want our service for Him. He doesn't want us going and going all day long, working for Him like a servant. No; this type of behavior stems from a "bondage mentality." What God wants is a love affair with His bride, *you and me*.

Jesus would leave His throne just to come to your home and visit with you.

He wants to spend time with you. He wants to be personal with you in the most spiritual way possible. He wants to fall in love with you today and then repeat that again tomorrow. He wants to be near to you. Jesus would leave His throne just to come to your home and visit with you. While you were sleeping, He would watch over you, and when you woke up, He would listen to what you have to say and then speak into your life in such a way that no other words would ever satisfy. Destiny dreaming is God the Father dreaming to be in everlasting communion with you.

Jesus would be engaged with everything you say and do from the moment you wake up until you went back to sleep that night. He would be right there waiting, listening, and watching to hear your voice and see your face just one more time for the day. That is how much Jesus loves you!

There isn't a greater love on earth than the love the Lord has for you. And this idea isn't something far off from another planet; it should be normal that God desires you. He passionately wants to be near you. Right now, His gentle arms are wide open and waiting for your embrace. You have an invitation to be with the King. And as you are starting to put your attention more towards the heart of the Father and His will for your life, He is releasing a divine romance over your life. He is imparting a love affair deep within your soul. This is destiny for your life. Destiny is calling out for you telling you to embrace the Father's love. Destiny says, "I love you, I want you, I need you."

> Let him kiss me with the kisses of his mouth—For your
> love is better than wine. (Song of Solomon 1:2)

Through Jesus There Is Complete Fullness

When we place Jesus first, He puts everything properly at His feet and then builds it back into our lives. He establishes systems, structures, and order in such a way that it creates a perfect peace deep within us—something that can't be destroyed unless we let it. He establishes the divine romance with us, where nothing else truly matters more than our Savior, Jesus Christ. It's at this stage where the former cares of this life are gone—vanished—and He is the center of all of our focus. This is destiny speaking!

> That I may know Him and the power of His resurrection,
> and the fellowship of His sufferings, being conformed
> to His death. (Philippians 3:10)

This amazing scripture is all about having a personal relationship with God. Paul realized that his life was most valuable only when he willed it over to Christ. Follow with me for a moment on Paul's train of thought. If we will our lives over to Christ, we surrender "us" for Him to take over. So to "know Christ" means to have a richer, more pure relationship with Him—an intimate relationship. The scripture goes on to teach us that this intimate relationship comes through participating in Christ's suffering, conforming to His death, experiencing the power of His resurrection, not only when we die, but by walking in His power while we are still on earth. This power isn't referring to resurrection power at our death; it's referring to having a personal relationship with Christ and having His resurrection power made manifest in and through our lives. My point? It's all about intimacy!

Paul uses the word *ginosko*, which refers to sexual intimacy. This is the same or almost the same word and meaning that was used when Mary the mother of Jesus said to the angel, "How can I have a child in my stomach when I haven't *known* a man yet?" What she was saying was, "How can I give birth to a child if I have not slept with, or had sex with, a man yet? Paul uses the similar Greek root word here to drive home a deep point when he said, "I want to *know* Christ." This is the deepest form of intimacy with Christ possible. It is a love affair with Christ (nothing immoral). It's a "love affair" where we are falling in love with Him at a level that's never been done within our lives.

Paul said "I want to have a love affair with Jesus." A what? What did you just say? A love affair with Jesus. That is what Paul was saying—and that is exactly what it means! The words specifically used are describing the most intimate relationship between a man and a woman. Of course, Paul wasn't saying it in the literal sense. Paul was driving home a huge point. The people of that time period would have caught on what he was saying. What Paul was really saying is, "I want to have a spiritual love affair—the deepest possible relationship ever. I want to have that relationship with Jesus Christ." They would have connected the wording Paul was using to describe how our relationship with God should be. To put it bluntly, it should be *very* personal and not a one-way relationship where all we do is get and take from God.

Our time with God is precious, and His time with us is, too. He wants this type of relationship with us—very intimate and personal. God desires this so much that He would love to be able to say about you, "YOU are a person after my own heart!" This is the type of love affair with Jesus that I'm talking about. It's nothing perverse or out of order, not dishonorable; it is strictly pure, honest, and loving in all ways.

This is Destiny's dream for you. It's destiny dreaming for you in more ways than one. You can go through any training seminar you want, but you can't have destiny until intimacy with God is the highest priority in your life. That is what the Apostle Paul is referring to here. A beautiful love affair with Jesus will cause you to desire Him more than anything else, and when you have a relationship like that, the troubles of this life become minor compared to the love of the Father and the power of His resurrection working in your life.

What Drives You?

There are many things in life that can drive a person: family matters, success, or personal hobbies, to name a few. For some, it's money, fortune, or fame. I'm around a lot of people who desire God and want to be involved more with ministry. I have seen ministers want to be so successful in ministry that it becomes their driving force in life. What drives you? What is it that keeps you moving more than anything else? Hopefully by now, you can answer this question—that answer is JESUS!

> Our driving force—our passion—
> must be our love for the Father.

As we have learned, our driving force—our passion—must be our love for the Father. His love is much greater than ours can ever be toward Him. That is the goodness and greatness of God. The idea that a king would come to live with you and me is simply crazy, but to those who love God, it's not. We see over and over again just how good He is toward us. That is the beauty of who God is. His goodness alone can be the greatest driving force in our lives. When I think about how good God is, especially when I don't deserve it, it really touches my heart and motivates me to honor and love Him more. But it wasn't always that way. There is another reason why I serve the Lord and really want to know Him more on a moment-by-moment basis. That is what I want to share with you next.

What Drives You to Love Jesus?

So what was it that drove me to Jesus? For me, it was a tragedy that turned into God's triumphant love and passion for my life. When

163

I saw how passionate God was for me combined with the fact that He chose to save me from overdosing, going to jail, and God knows whatever else could have happened as I was doing drugs and partying all the time, I knew I owed it to Him to serve Him the rest of my life. But I want to point out something here: owing my life to Him was my free will and choice. He never once demanded that I serve Him like a master does to a slave. From the start, this relationship was a progressive path to intimacy with my Father. The bottom line is that I just fell in love with Him—because of who He is more so than any other reason.

That thought brings me to one more thing.

Don't Ever Give Up on Those You Love and Care For

Maybe there are people around you who don't understand the love God has for them yet. Don't give up on them! This love affair is for all who gather into the arms of God. He wants everyone in His loving arms, to fall in love with Him. This includes the people who are close to your heart but far away from His. He is just as passionate for them as He is for you. Sometimes we forget that this divine romance can affect everyone around us. As they see the love of the Father working through us, they will want what we have—a love affair with Jesus. The Lord wants all of you, and then He wants your entire family. But He's not stopping there. After He gets all of your family, then He wants your entire neighborhood. He wants to love on everyone who surrounds your life, and He wants to work through you to show them something they desperately need to have. It doesn't matter what your family is facing or what the person down the street is involved in; God wants to break open the bondages that are holding them back. He wants to pour His saving grace over their lives. God loves them, and He won't stop until He gets them back.

When we fall in love with God, the intimacy that is established will help us love the people around us even more. The more I fell in love with Christ, the more I loved my mother and father. I also started to see those around me the way Christ was seeing them—

broken and empty without God. This changed my perspective on how I treated my co-workers and friends.

One tiny taste of the goodness of God can cause the most evil person to turn and come running back to the Father.

I want to encourage you to keep praying for your family and loved ones. Don't stop, no matter how bad their lives get. Believe that they will see a powerful breakthrough in their lives and that they will experience the divine romance with the Father. All it takes is one supernatural encounter with God. Just one tiny taste of the goodness of God can cause the most evil person to turn and come running back to the Father. His love is stronger than any drug ever known. His mercy runs deeper than any depth in the ocean. We cannot outrun or escape the Father's intimate love for us. I believe that as you fall deeper in love with God, this divine romance will spread like a holy fire into your family, your friends, and your community. I expect to hear amazing stories about it all!

CHAPTER 15: A CHECKLIST FOR YOUR DESTINY

Have you ever read a book, sat in on a class, or heard some amazing teaching on a topic that really resonated with your spirit? I mean, it really hit you deep down inside, like God was setting you up for that exact moment so that He could speak to you. It was crystal clear, but the ending felt like it was cut short. You got all fired up, excited and ready to move forward, but something was missing. You got the "Why you need to change" part, but they left out the most important element; the "How you need to go about changing" wasn't given. In those cases, moving forward is completely on your own.

This happens a lot, both in the world and in the church. Catching the vision is the easy part; following through with something is much harder. For example, it has been said that out of all the New Year's resolutions that people make in January, only 8% of those people follow through with them.

Destiny dreams for you. Destiny wants you to be part of that 8% by the end of this year—the people who have followed through with God's call and vision for your life. This is the heart of the Father for you. He wants you to succeed and make progress in life.

The truest form of teaching is leading someone through the process from start to finish. It's not about just giving people information or a great message, praying for them, and moving on, never to be involved with their lives again. That's the reason I wrote this chapter: to be in your life just a little bit more and to help you out a little bit further with your destiny. Finding and walking in your destiny is important for everyone, and following through and finishing your destiny is most important. This doesn't come fast, it won't just fall in your lap, and it certainly doesn't come through happenstance. Destiny is appointed by God, given through God, and it is followed through with our obedience in walking with the Lord.

> # Finding and walking in your destiny is important for everyone, and following through and finishing your destiny is most important.

Now that you have come this far, I want to make sure that I leave you with something that will help you along the way. I want to give you something to walk through life with. Maybe you don't necessarily need a course change in your life, a new job, or a different church, but you know you need to shift a few things. How you got right here will not be how you move forward in your destiny.

What you're about to read and go through next can seem elementary for some people, and it could be challenging for others. This is the goal, the purpose of adding this section to the book. I want to make sure that you are challenged to take your walk with God seriously. I'm passionate about presence with Jesus, and I want you to be, too. I'm serious about destiny and how it works, and I believe that now you are, too. For this reason, I want to give you something for your journeys ahead. I have created a practical checklist for you to help you find and walk in your destiny. First, I will explain how you should be looking at and the perspective needed for answering the questions, and then the actual checklist will follow on page 177. Feel free to write your answers down, and use a notebook if you need more space to answer the questions.

The Checklist for Destiny Explained

The No-boundaries Goal

The first question of the checklist asks this: If there were no boundaries at all, no cost factors, no hurdles to jump, mountains to climb, or fences to cut through, what would you want to be in life? The following question asks if that goal is actually attainable for you.

It's easy for most of us to rattle off what we would love to do if we had all the money and resources and following in the world. What's important to consider is if this is actually attainable.

For example, a 3'9" fully grown man will probably not end up in the professional football or basketball leagues. I'm not saying that they can't get there; we all know of exceptions to the rule. I'm just saying that more than likely, they won't, because their physical body would dictate that is not going to be what they will excel at. Likewise, a professional sumo wrestler most likely won't be able to quit their career and win an Olympic triathlon within the same year.

We all believe in the supernatural, and the examples above would really be supernatural and require God to really work in amazing ways; however, there are natural laws and principles set in place by God Himself that He will sometimes use to guide a person and help them into their destiny.

Just for fun, let's look at another example: a ninety-year-old individual will probably not apply to become the president of the United States. And if they do, they will likely have a hard time acquiring that goal in life. Why? Age does matter. Health does, too.

With that said, ask yourself if your dream job or calling is truly attainable. There is a huge difference between following your God-appointed destiny by faith and stepping out in blind fate, attempting to do something that sounds "supernatural," but in reality is just done out of ignorance or stubbornness. There are times when God gives us something to do that other people think is crazy, and when it is truly from the Lord, things will fall into place to see it be accomplished. Other times, we are being led by our own selfish motivations (and we like to wrap them up in spiritual packages to make them seem like God's will). We have to be able to discern what is from God and what is from us.

Sometimes there is a dream we have and God says no, and sometimes He will refuse to give you the answer that you want to hear. The heart of the matter is this: If your destiny "dream job" position, location, path, or course in life is truly from the Lord, then regardless of how far off it may seem, it is attainable.

> If your destiny "dream job" position, location, path, or course in life is truly from the Lord, then regardless of how far off it may seem, it is attainable.

Accountability and Hearing the Voice of the Lord

The third question on the checklist deals with figuring out who you are accountable to. Having godly people around me to keep me accountable has been one of the best things for my life. Through the years, I've kept people in my life who are willing to listen and speak directly into the situations I have faced. Having people in your life to help direct you during tough times is extremely important. Also having certain coaches in your life is also important. Here are a few of the types of mentors you should have:

- A pastor or a spiritual mentor (this could be your spiritual mother or father)
- A coach (ministry, writing, business) or counselor

Your spiritual mentor is a person or couple who have been in the ministry and are called to pastor or shepherd people. They might be pastors in a local church or overseers of other ministries. These are people who are truly concerned for your wellbeing. They will be honest and upfront when needed, as well as compassionate and loving. They will help direct your life in such a way that you will grow immensely under their leadership. If you are a minister, this needs to be more than just having a license or ordination paper saying that you have a person overseeing your life who you never see and barely talk to; this is a lifetime or long-term commitment from someone who is willing to live and walk out life together with other people. They have been in life situations that you deal with before you and can give you guidance when needed.

Having a coach or counselor is also crucial. I'm often asked why it is needed. Think about it this way. Professional athletes all have professional coaches. Although the teams practice, train, and play together regularly, each individual player will learn and grow at their own pace. Some are going to understand things that others won't, and one way to get as many people on the team working together well is to have personal athletic trainers. These trainers are able to work one-on-one with the players to work out tough challenges some of them might be experiencing. This helps them excel in what they can do best at a later time.

This is the same way having a coach or counselor works in God's kingdom. For example, when I knew that it was time to write this book, I hired a writing coach. A what? A writing coach. This individual helped me with the book from beginning to end. They gave me advice about what should and shouldn't be in a book, which was very helpful for me, as a first-time author. They also walked me through the entire writing and publishing process, which gave me a greater understanding for the vision of this book and even also for the future vision of other books. My writing coach helped me recognize what parts of this book needed to be explained more, focused on less, or even placed in another book at a later time.

At crucial stages in life, sometimes we just need to have a "life coach" or a specialized coach "mentor" who will help us shift properly in the right direction. Sometimes, a certain coach is seasonal for what you are doing at a certain time in your life. You might need a business coach one year, and later on you might need a writing or ministry coach.

They may be regulars, or they might come and go. Either way, they are important to help you walk in genuine destiny.

Trusted friends

Did you realize that one of the greatest kings who ever lived had a close friend? King David and Jonathan, Saul's son, were close friends, yet God specifically said about David, that he was, "A man after My heart."

> But now your kingdom shall not continue. The Lord has sought for Himself a man after His own heart, and the Lord has commanded him to be commander over His people, because you have not kept what the Lord commanded you. (1 Samuel 13:14)

King David is the only person in the Bible who God said that about, so why would King David need anything else but God? Wouldn't that be enough? How big is God's heart? You might wonder why he would need anything else at all. Because *relationships* are crucial to our destiny!

God is relational. His heart is that we would have relationships toward each other in the body of Christ. God never called you to fly solo. He doesn't want you to walk alone and battle everything that you're going to fight all by yourself. Even God brought Jonathan into King David's life as a close friend.

You've probably heard it said before: "Everything works through relationships." This is certainly true! Without relationships properly placed within your life, you will not be divinely connected to the body of Christ. If you're not connected, your life will be disjointed and out of sync, which is *not* God's will for your life.

Friends can change. Friends come and go. Friends can also betray you. But God has called a friend—a genuine, true, and trusted friend into your life. There might be seasons in your life where you feel led to walk alone for a while. This is normal; even Jesus went up away by Himself to the mountain to be completely alone. There are seasons in our lives that we will be "called up and called out" in order to be alone with God. But being alone won't last forever. That is why I ask who your most trusted friends are.

Figuring out who your three most trusted friends are is so important for your destiny.

Figuring out who your three most trusted friends are is so important for your destiny. In fact, if you truly can't say honestly that you have all three, you should really pray and believe for God to send you these three trusted friends quickly. This is one of the most important parts of your checklist for destiny. Once you have these first four questions answered, you can move on to the final question.

The Next Steps

> For which of you, intending to build a tower, does not sit down first and count the cost, whether he has enough to finish it? (Luke 14:28)

When you're building a house, one of the first steps is completing the blueprints. This is the road map for how the house will be built. Building a home is somewhat like developing a blueprint for your life. If your destiny involves being a fireman, you're probably going to have to finish high school first. Secondly, you will most likely become a volunteer fireman while you are getting extensive training in the field. Likewise, you will probably have to get certified in CPR and acquire other skills or take classes that involve becoming and maintaining your fireman status. Now fast-forward a few years. Maybe you're reading this right now and you're already a fireman, but God has placed it on your heart to become a firetruck driver in some of the toughest and most dangerous places in your city. Now He is leading you to step it up. You're going to have to get further training, probably take some

173

tests, and also become certified. Maybe your certification will require recertification each year, which means further studies or testing along the way. Do you follow the path here? Each destiny is unique, different, yet sovereign in God's design.

So what is God telling you to do next? That is the final question for the checklist, and it is so important to give it careful thought before writing down your answer.

Think about this in the bigger picture. For instance, God spoke to me about leaving my father's business one day in order to go into my destiny. It just didn't happen overnight. It was a long process and required a lot of praying, thinking it through, and timing. God didn't say to me, "Sal, I want you to stop doing business and construction with your father and leave him high and dry tomorrow." One of the first steps for me was to talk to my father. I felt the Lord tell me that I needed to give my dad a two-year notice. Why? Because I was the one my dad was going to eventually hand over the company to one day. And at the time, I really depended on him and he really depended on me; we both needed each other a lot, and God understood this, so He was willing to work with the situation.

> ## Destiny isn't always a quick or abrupt step in life. Often it is a subtle, well-planned-out course adjustment.

Destiny isn't always a quick or abrupt step in life. Often it is a subtle, well-planned-out course adjustment. Something life-changing does not always have to include a bizarre and sudden jump. If I would have just left my dad's company with a two-week notice, it would have both dishonored him and wounded him deeply. God saw this and He respects it because He is a God of honor. He wouldn't ask you to do something that He wouldn't honor through the process. Looking back now, leaving my father's company has really helped my relationship with him and my mother. We have all grown to appreciate and respect each other more. When I visit with my dad now, it's not a work relationship; it's more like a father-son relationship—how it's supposed to be.

Now you can proceed to the checklist. Are you able to answer each of the questions? If not, which areas are missing? It is really important to map out a blueprint for your life. This will help you set a course that will keep you on track for the things you have to do to fulfill your destiny, which is walking in God's plan for your life. It will take time, effort, and hard work. We have to come to a place where we are willing to take time to think it through and plan it out. I have heard that people spend more time planning their vacations than planning out their life goals. Don't let this be you! Spend time often to plan out where you believe God is taking you.

THE CHECKLIST FOR DESTINY

1. If there were no boundaries at all, no cost factors, no hurdles to jump, mountains to climb, or fences to cut through, what would you want to be in life?

_____

_____

_____

2. Is this goal really attainable?

_____

_____

_____

3. Who are three people in life you are accountable to?

_____

_____

_____

4. Who are your most trusted friends?

_____

_____

_____

5. What is God telling you to do next in life?

_____

_____

_____

CONCLUSION

How do you sum up the love of the Father? As much as we would like to try, we really can't. We can search out God's mind, will, and thoughts for the rest of eternity, and we still will only be scratching the surface of the depth of His love toward the human race. As much as we profess to have "attained" the fullness and greatness of the love of the Father, we haven't.

The fact is that we will not reach the fullness of Christ until we come into the fullness of Christ with Him in eternity. That is the hope that you and I carry; that is the promise God has for us. We can search the Scriptures and study the heart of God for the rest of our lives, and there is still more to discover! This shows us just how awesome our Father in heaven is. Nobody can attain perfect knowledge about any one topic about God, because nobody can ever be God. No one person can ever have the complete mind of God because that would make us "like God," which is how we all got into this mess at the beginning of creation.

God never wanted us to be "like God." He wants us to carry His image and His glory, and *be* His image. That doesn't mean that we are becoming like God in the sense that we are little "gods" walking around. The purpose of you and I being crafted in His image is based on the Father's love for us. We have been given the breath of life to carry out His will for our lives to the nations. This is His pleasing and acceptable will for us. He wants us to be ambassadors of love. He wants us to be His hands, His feet, and mainly His heart to those

179

who are in need of help. That is what makes the divine romance with God so special. He wants you to reflect Him to those who don't know Him at all.

There really is no greater calling or gift that can ever be given to you than the gift of salvation. Just the thought that God Himself came down and died a horrible death on a cross to save your soul is beyond comprehension. Maybe you heard this before, but it is the truth: He died for you, and if you were the only one on earth, Jesus wouldn't have turned back from the death of the cross. He did it for you!

But then it gets deeper! Not only did God send His Son to take the place of your sin, He also gave you His kingdom heart and a divine breath of destiny tucked deep within you, just waiting to be released and revealed. He planted inside of you a love from the Father like no other love ever known on earth. This is a deep love filled with awe, grace, mercy, and compassion toward the unforgivable and the unlovable.

This love is eternal—something that grows stronger through time.

But it still goes deeper than that! This love doesn't weaken in time like a long-lost bond with an old friend, or like a memory that grows too hazy to recall. This love is eternal—something that grows stronger through time. It's an undying love that causes the blind to see, the deaf to hear, and the dead to rise. It's what causes a baby to take its first breath and the dying widow to take her last. From beginning to end, God's love never fades in our lives. His divine romance gets better and better as the days go by. Your walk with God is the best walk you will ever have in life! This is how I want you to see destiny dreams. Destiny is dreaming for you.

CONCLUSION

A Checklist for Intimacy

Last but not least, I want to leave you with one more checklist. For some who have been doing this already, it may seem very basic. That's okay! You should still look over this and see if there are any areas in which you might be lacking. Sometimes we feel as though we've arrived with something God has given us, when in actuality, we are just starting to learn something all over again so God can show us a new side of things.

Have you ever read a scripture a hundred times, and then suddenly something will jump right out at you? After all those times, you now see the revelation of what it's really all about. This is how intimacy with the Father can work; it will change, shift, grow, and mature until we are with Him in eternity. Then it all starts over again, but better this time. Regardless of where your walk is with the Lord, intimacy takes time and effort to cultivate, so I want to make sure that you have something to take with you.

Intimacy Requires These Things on a Regular Basis:

- **Reading God's Word.** Reading and studying faithfully is a must when it comes to maturing with God.

- **Spending time with God through prayer.** Prayer is talking to Him, not just giving Him a prayer request or list, but talking with Him and *listening*.

- **Fasting.** Fasting is important, but please do research and talk to your doctor before you start a fast. Fasting must be God-led and it's something that can change your walk with God immensely. However, if it is not done right, it can damage your body. So please talk with God and your medical doctor if you have never fasted before, or if you're not sure how it works.

- **Gatherings.** It doesn't matter where you gather to worship and learn about the Bible; what matters most is what is happening while you are gathering with other people. Size doesn't matter in this situation, so find a church where you can be welcomed and fit into it the way you are designed to function in the body of Christ.

- **Worship.** Worship isn't just done in church on a Sunday morning. You don't even have to be gathered with other people or even have music. Sing to God. Worship Him out of the overflow of thankfulness for what He has done for you.

- **Praying in the Spirit.** What better way to have intimacy with God than to speak a language that only He can understand? Your spiritual tongue is unique to you, and the Holy Spirit prays things through you on a level that goes beyond the natural.

- **Keep a journal.** There are many things you can record in a journal that apply to intimacy with God. You can write down dreams or visions that you have so you don't forget them. Write a love letter to Jesus, or record experiences that you have in His presence, or even things He speaks to you throughout your day. Keep it close because you won't believe how often He actually speaks to you!

- **Silence.** As important as it is to pray, it's equally—if not even more—crucial to take time to listen to what God is saying to us. We can only do this by being still and tuning everything else in our lives out so His voice is the only one we hear at the moment.

I hope this list has helped you. Please feel free to contact me. I would love to hear more about God's destiny for your life and how it's all unfolding.

ABOUT THE AUTHOR

S al Cerra's life and ministry is marked by supernatural experiences with God, visions, revelations, and visitations. Having been through fiery trials throughout his life, both Sal and his wife, Kristine, are living testimonies of God's promise of restoration. Together they founded Destiny Fire Ministries and have a heart for seeing people set free from bondage and past struggles. Their desire is for people to see themselves for who they really are—true sons and daughters of a loving heavenly Father, able to walk in the fullness they were created for, which will cultivate the deep intimacy with God that every believer can have.

Since Sal first began walking with God, his deepest longing has been to understand what genuine intimacy and true sonship really looks like. Through his years in business and ministry, this desire for intimacy with God has led him in a desperate pursuit of the Father's heart. The focus of Sal's message is to help people know who the Father really is, which leads to them falling in love with Jesus, experiencing levels of God's grace, and discovering their true identity as sons and daughters of God.

Sal was not only involved with his family's business for twenty-five years, but had also owned his own construction business for twenty years concurrently. He completed four years of schooling about ministry and the supernatural. Sal and Kristine have six children and one grandchild, and live in Central New York with their two youngest children. Sal can be contacted at destiny@destinyfire.org or from his website: www.destinyfire.org.

183

Sal + Kristine Cerra
Sal's cell - (315) 641-3626